"This is a must-read book on leadership. Fresh in its perspective and personal in its style, it will appeal to both millennials and baby boomers at the same time. I could not put the book down."

— *Prasad Kaipa, leadership consultant and educator, and co-author of* From Smart to Wise *and* You Can.

"Research shows that people learn best from stories and experiential narratives. *Letters to A Young Leader* is a terrific example of how everyday storytelling and first-hand experiences can drive important lessons among young professionals. It's a must-read for anyone engaged in a growing and dynamic organization."

— *Robert Rodriguez, founder and CEO of Cambria Solutions (IT)*

"Denhardt has proven once again that he can provide valuable insights on leadership that advance our understanding of the modern workplace. *Letters to a Young Leader* is a book we especially need in these times."

— *Jay Hakes, former director of the Jimmy Carter Presidential Library*

LETTERS TO A YOUNG LEADER

If you are interested in becoming a better leader, this book is a great place to start. Rather than using the familiar textbook approach, leadership expert Robert Denhardt offers practical lessons drawn from a lively year-long correspondence with two (fictional) former students about their experiences in leadership.

The letters explore the deeply personal issues these and other young and emerging leaders are facing – what the skills and personal qualities are that you need for contemporary leadership, what leadership will mean to you and those you lead, and even why you might or might not want to become a leader. Along the way, the book speaks to the big picture, arguing that leadership today has been stripped of its historic contribution to creating meaningful human experience and has been reduced to a technical exercise in executive management.

Based on his experience of teaching leadership to thousands of undergraduates, graduate students, and advanced practitioners, Denhardt speaks person-to-person with young leaders about their questions and their concerns as they enter into the somewhat flawed world of leadership today. The result is a call for a new leadership for a new generation.

This book will be valuable to students enrolled in regular and executive degree programs in leadership, business management, public administration, nonprofit management, educational administration, and many other fields. It also speaks to young leaders out of school but committed to enhancing their leadership. Indeed, readers of all ages will learn lessons relevant to their own professional development.

Robert B. Denhardt is a central figure in leadership education and currently heads Denhardt Leadership, a boutique consulting and publishing firm. He was Professor and Director of Leadership Programs in the Sol Price School of Public Policy at the University of Southern California, USA.

LETTERS TO A YOUNG LEADER

A New Leadership for a New Generation

Robert B. Denhardt

NEW YORK AND LONDON

First published 2020
by Routledge
52 Vanderbilt Avenue, New York, NY 10017

and by Routledge
2 Park Square, Milton Park, Abingdon, Oxon, OX14 4RN

Routledge is an imprint of the Taylor & Francis Group, an informa business

© 2020 Taylor & Francis

The right of Robert B. Denhardt to be identified as author of this work has been asserted by him in accordance with sections 77 and 78 of the Copyright, Designs and Patents Act 1988.

All rights reserved. No part of this book may be reprinted or reproduced or utilised in any form or by any electronic, mechanical, or other means, now known or hereafter invented, including photocopying and recording, or in any information storage or retrieval system, without permission in writing from the publishers.

Trademark notice: Product or corporate names may be trademarks or registered trademarks, and are used only for identification and explanation without intent to infringe.

Library of Congress Cataloging-in-Publication Data
A catalog record for this title has been requested

ISBN: 9780367243999 (hbk)
ISBN: 9780367244002 (pbk)
ISBN: 9780429285042 (ebk)

Typeset in Bembo
by Apex CoVantage, LLC

To my students, my teachers

A WALK

My eyes already touch the sunny hill.
going far beyond the road I have begun,
So we are grasped by what we cannot grasp;
it has an inner light, even from a distance-

and changes us, even if we do not reach it,
into something else, which, hardly sensing it,
we already are; a gesture waves us on
answering our own wave . . .
but what we feel is the wind in our faces.

–Rainer Maria Rilke

CONTENTS

Introduction		*xv*
1	Letter from Bob: August 21	1
2	Letter from Kayla: September 5	5
3	Letter from Mike: September 12	9
4	Letter from Bob: October 2	12
5	Letter from Kayla: October 14	18
6	Letter from Mike: October 20	20
7	Letter from Bob: October 31	23
8	Letter from Bob: November 5	30
9	Letter from Kayla: November 10	37
10	Letter from Mike: November 20	39
11	Letter from Bob: December 10	41

12	Letter from Kayla: December 14	50
13	Letter from Mike: December 15	52
14	Letter from Bob: January 15	54
15	Letter from Bob: January 20	61
16	Letter from Mike: January 22	65
17	Letter from Bob: January 25	66
18	Letter from Bob: January 30	72
19	Letter from Kayla: February 2	80
20	Letter from Mike: February 12	83
21	Letter from Bob: February 20	86
22	Letter from Kayla: February 25	93
23	Letter from Mike: February 27	95
24	Letter from Bob: March 8	96
25	Letter from Bob: April 2	101
26	Letter from Bob: April 12	107
27	Letter from Bob: April 14	113
28	Letter from Kayla: May 1	119
29	Letter from Mike: May 5	121
30	Letter from Bob: May 15	124
31	Letter from Bob: May 20	132
32	Letter from Kayla: June 1	137

33	Letter from Bob: June 8	139
34	Letter from Mike: June 21	145
35	Letter from Kayla: July 3	147
36	Letter from Mike: July 16	149
37	Letter from Bob: July 18	151
38	Letter from Bob: July 21	153

Endnotes *163*
A Reader's Guide to the Literature on Leadership *167*
Bibliography and Works Cited *172*
Acknowledgments *176*
Index *179*

INTRODUCTION

> Learning to lead is about learning to learn. And learning to learn is about the whole person. The only way to become a better leader is to become a better person.

About a year ago, after the last of our advanced leadership classes, two of my students, whom I'll call Kayla and Mike, walked with me toward the Lab, a bar and restaurant just across from campus, for our usual after-class "debriefing." Our minds were still spinning from an especially intense class discussion about the challenges facing young and emerging leaders today.

Many students said that they felt out of the mainstream of organizational life today, some feeling excluded by their more senior co-workers, others expressing an unwillingness to engage in practices that seemed inconsistent with their values. But there were lots of questions and a lively, even stormy debate ensued. A calming drink sounded just right.

As we talked and revisited some of the ideas people had put forward, Kayla asked whether I had ever gathered some of my ideas and my students' responses in written form to share with others. I had not.

We began to imagine a collection of lecture notes, reflections on leadership, and critical observations about leadership as it will play out in the lives of today's developing leaders. The content should not be abstract but should address *the personal experiences and values of the emerging leaders themselves.* Within this context, we would also *consider the limitations of the current idea of leadership and encourage young leaders to take on the challenge of constructing and putting into practice a new leadership for a new generation.*

For some reason, we began to call the proposed exchanges "letters" – even though they would probably be e-mail attachments. I liked the idea, even though the term "letters" sounded a little old-fashioned.

But letters can be personal, even intimate; they can be cautious or purely speculative; and they can be addressed to a single individual or, as it turned out here, to more than one. They also provide the opportunity for the writer to be more thoughtful, more reflective, and more expansive than in e-mails or, certainly, in texts. And they always imply a back-and-forth, a conversation.

After our drinks arrived, Mike wondered whether he and Kayla might help by responding to my letters, based on their own experiences as emerging leaders. He pointed out that this could also help them by continuing our mentoring relationship. I thought this was a wonderful idea, and offered to write the first letter, giving my understanding of what we were undertaking and posing some questions to get us started.

1
LETTER FROM BOB
August 21

Dear Kayla and Mike,

Since we talked a few weeks ago, I've thought a lot about how to frame our conversations, and especially about how I can be most helpful to you.

I could follow the popular road, one well traveled by executive coaches, consultants, columnists, and bloggers, and offer practical advice on what you should do to be "successful" – that is how you, as an emerging leader, can work your way to the top of your organization . . . and stay there.

There's plenty of speaking and writing of this type, and frankly, while I find some of it helpful, much of it seems somewhat "scripted" and a little hollow. Typically, the writer/commentator will identify a problem, present several solutions (either numbered or called "secrets" or both), then urge the reader to follow these nuggets of advice with the promise of significant professional rewards.

The titles for these lessons often follow a familiar pattern, such as "Ten Ways to Cultivate New Partnerships," or "Five Minds of the Millennial." (You can substitute three or five or seven, though rarely four or six or eight – other than ten, even numbers don't seem to fare well in the virtual world).

If the title doesn't contain numbers, it at least implies an offer to let the reader in on something hidden from others – for example, "The Secrets of Slow Marketing." The "secrets" may be preceded by a number (e.g., "Three Secrets . . ."), but it always implies something hush-hush and is typically followed by a phrase no one has ever heard before – such as "Slow Marketing." (I made up that term, then discovered there is such a thing!)

The content that follows in these works is generally common sense dressed up in clever phrases or slogans, such as one of mine: "You must learn to be uncomfortable with the comfortable," that is, if you get too complacent, others will pass you by. The key phrase is always written or spoken in knowing tones and always repeated at least once. The ideas are always memorable, just as pictures are, but they are usually vague and of limited use in real life. My advice then is – don't read columns or posts that have either numbers or the word "secrets" in the title – not even mine!

Rather than providing such guideposts along the road to "success" as a leader, I think I can be helpful in a different way – *by working with you to provide perspective, to put leadership into context.* By this I mean considering not just the skills of leadership, the techniques, but thinking about how your leadership affects you, how it affects those close to you, and how it affects the broader community. I hope we can sort through the way that leadership builds from inside, exposing what Parker Palmer calls "the leader within."

That process, the personal work of leading, is not easy; it takes a great deal of self-reflection, self-critique, and self-understanding. There will be days that yield great insight and excitement, and days you feel barren and resentful. But don't despair. Your persistence and resilience will carry you forward.

In contrast to the hype and pretense typical of many discussions of leadership today, I hope we can model a sincere, thoughtful, insightful, and, most of all, caring way of talking about leadership. I hope we can focus less on the noisy world of power in which many so-called leaders reside and more on the quiet confidence that shines from within the best leaders, allowing them to connect with others in a way that energizes them and causes them to act.

I hope we can also strive for clarity and simplicity in our words and ideas. That doesn't mean that our discussion needs to be simplistic. Rather, we need to understand the subject deeply, but then draw out the essential meaning of the terms we use and the activities we describe. Albert Einstein is often quoted as saying: "If you can't explain it simply, you don't understand it well enough." I hope we can come to understand leadership sufficiently to explain it in simple terms. And I hope that the resulting clarity in our thinking about leadership will carry over into your practices as a leader and those of many others in your generation and beyond.

Many young leaders (the two of you are exceptions) accept without question the current model of leadership and are not willing to engage in critiques of that model. It's not that they actively defend the model, but in leadership, as in everything else, we often depend on "the way we've always done it."

But the way we've always done leadership may no longer be acceptable. While the traditional approach to leadership in organizations has benefitted many, there have been serious and mounting negative consequences as well.

I think that we are at a crucial turning point in the study and practice of leadership. The way you and other young leaders conceive of leadership, and the way that you model leadership over the next fifty years or so will set a pattern that may be followed for centuries to come. That's why it's important that we get this right.

Images of Leadership

It's important to begin by examining the ideas we have in our heads and the feelings we have in our hearts about leading. Of course, we already know that interpretations of leadership can be elusive and range from the mystical to the mundane. The practice of leadership contains elements of both — and everything in between. Leadership remains an enigma: we know leadership when we see it, but we're not sure what it is, and we're not sure how to get it.

Some think of leadership as something people are either born with or not. Others think leadership can be developed either through experience or through education or both. Some think leadership primarily involves skills or techniques such as creating a vision, communicating the vision, and motivating others to pursue that vision. Others see leadership as dependent on more personal qualities such as courage, empathy, tolerance, and patience. Still others emphasize the importance of ethics and values in leadership.

Despite this confusion, leadership continues to be a popular, almost faddish topic. The shelves of any large chain bookstore — if you can still find one — are filled with literally hundreds if not thousands of texts, biographies, and self-help books on leadership. Meanwhile, television commentators and social media "experts" call for more effective and responsible leadership in our country and around the world. Yet despite all the books and articles that have been written about leadership, despite all the discussions, leadership remains hard to understand and even harder to practice.

Now, I'm not one who believes that all the ills of the world can be solved by improved leadership. Many people seem to hold that point of view, and that probably contributes to the faddishness of the topic. Indeed, those in what Barbara Kellerman calls the "leadership industry" — leadership consultants, executive coaches, retired military and corporate executives, and scholars who teach and write about leadership — have probably oversold their product, especially in comparison to the limited impact they can have on the development of individual leaders and the limited effect leadership by itself can have on society. (Society is probably moved as much by accident, failure, miscommunications, and pure luck as by leadership.)

This is not to say that leadership is unimportant. To the contrary, leadership is a significant factor in achieving important goals and in shaping the quality of our experience in groups, organizations, communities, and societies. Leaders help us find purpose and direction, they provide a sense of security, and they help us cope with uncertainty, confusion, and change. Leadership is important, and worthy of careful thought and diligent practice. But it's not all-important. So, let's be realistic about both its opportunities and its limitations.

What Can You Expect of Me?

After years of working with students moving into public, private, and nonprofit organizations, while at the same time managing and (hopefully) leading in various settings, I've witnessed both the possibilities and the limitations of leadership. I've experienced personally both the highs and the lows of leading.

So, when someone says that they are confronting roadblocks and frustration in trying to lead, or that leading is like sailing in rough seas, I can relate to that. I can empathize – at least in part. But that doesn't mean I nor we can "fix it." Our discussions are not likely to eliminate the ups and downs of life in organizations and in leadership, but I do hope that we will be able to smooth the seas a little. And we should be able to point the direction in which future interpretations of leadership should move. In fact, I think we must!

To get us started, maybe each of you could write about the path that you are on in your leadership journey and identify some of the potential bumps you have encountered along the way. At the same time, you might talk about some of the opportunities that you see ahead of you. That should be helpful in starting and "grounding" our discussion!

Thanks for your help! I'm really looking forward to our discussions!

Yours,

Bob

2
LETTER FROM KAYLA

September 5

Dr. Denhardt

I'm excited to be involved in the "letters" project and hope I can be helpful. You asked Mike and me to begin by describing some of the opportunities and challenges we have encountered in our workplaces.

I'm only a few years out of school and new to the consulting business, but I think I landed a really good job. The people I work with most closely, my peers, are smart and hard-working. Of course, most are technical folks (while my degree is in sociology with a minor in management). But our teams include people from various disciplines and, for the most part, that works just fine. We learn a lot from one another.

I've also found that this company, and especially its CEO, Robert, provides many development opportunities for younger employees, something that is especially important to me and others of my generation. I think I will learn a lot while I'm here and this experience will provide a good stepping-stone for advancing my career.

Don't get me wrong – there are problems that arise from time to time. This place is not perfect. Some of the difficulties involve tension between our younger employees and some of the more senior managers. Others arise from differences in the way people of all ages approach their work: some seem to get real joy and satisfaction from what they're doing, while others are just putting in the hours. Finally, there are occasional issues of sexism and gender discrimination that really bother me.

There have been some things that have surprised me, both about the organization and about myself. I'll mention three.

First, I remember a human resources training session on "diversity" we had shortly after I got here. We were talking in groups about bringing different perspectives to the workplace. The conversation was pretty much what you would expect, until the representative of one group stood up and spent his entire time criticizing the "millennials" who worked in the company.

He described the millennials, my generation, as self-absorbed, lazy, and apathetic, having short attention spans, and as incapable of commitment. It was all negative, extremely so, and delivered in a very demeaning tone – at least that's the way I heard it.

I was debating whether to stand up and object. But, being the youngest and newest person in the room, I hesitated. Happily, another group's representative spoke up, reporting that her group also talked about millennials, but that they had a more positive view. She described our generation as having a strong sense of social responsibility, as being creative, innovative, and imaginative, as well as having the flexibility to move easily from one workplace to another.

Since I happened to be the only millennial in the group, several people encouraged me to speak. I was hesitant to do so, but I had to say something. I pointed out that millennials prefer quality rather than quantity in their work (and are willing to be selective), they seek jobs that give them a sense of meaning and a degree of autonomy (and are likely to move on if they don't find it), and they want to be recognized as individuals, rather than stereotyped as representative of their generation. A few others agreed, and still others disagreed. I went home that evening feeling a little depressed, not that I didn't hold my own, but that the conversation even had to take place. Why so much drama?

Second, my niece, Olivia, who is 9 years old, spent a week with my husband and me a couple of months ago. Olivia likes to draw and, during her visit, spent many hours with her sketchpad. One picture that she drew of me showed my face with a happy expression on the left side but a dark, almost fearful expression on the right. When I asked about the sketch, Olivia told me that each day I came home with a different look on my face, so when she drew me I needed more than one face.

I thought the picture reflected the emotional roller coaster of my first few years with the company. I expected that graduating from college and starting into my career would put me in a happy place, and sometimes it does, but the days are mixed. Maybe the picture was connected to the generational differences I talked about earlier. Maybe it was a reaction to the different styles of management that I encounter. Maybe it reflects gender discrimination in the company, which is subtle but still a part of our culture.

I think I would feel better if someone would just say, "Kayla, you're doing a good job!" But they rarely do – and I don't get it. It requires so little effort to be nice to people. I mean, how much time does it take to say to someone that they're doing good job? Apparently too much for some.

Several of the managers around here spend their time so worried about the structure of the organization and their own positions that they are not concerned with building relationships with their employees, or their clients for that matter. It's like there is this "hidden force" that keeps them confined to playing a certain role and keeping a certain distance. They don't take the time to really get to know others and they sometimes get burned by it. But they continue to engage in the same behavior – again and again, walking right into the fire.

What about me? I seem to be doing the work well, but I don't yet feel comfortable and secure. I have this feeling of being just a little out of step, and it's very disconcerting, especially when I dare to think of myself as being on a path to leadership.

I talk almost every night with my mother, who had a long career as a corporate executive. She suggested it might be related to organizational culture, that I haven't found the "rhythm" of the organization and how I fit in. But for me, it's an identity thing – I'm concerned about how I can maintain my own identity and yet make a mark in this organization.

I guess there is considerable tension between these two ideas. The organization wants me to fit in and probably even needs me to do so. I might even be more comfortable that way. But I want to stand out and probably even need to do so. And, ironically, the organization even needs some people to be a little unusual (progressive?). Maybe that tension is what Olivia saw in my face and was trying to draw.

Finally, and I just can't even believe this ... We were gathering for the kick-off meeting of a new project team. There were several men in the room; I was the only woman. The project director, Howard Clark, a man I had met only briefly once before, was settling into his chair at the front of the room. Howard was known for having a story or a joke for every occasion. And almost every story he told had an ending demeaning to minorities or women. I disliked him from the beginning.

Just as I was putting my tablet down, Howard saw me and, with something between a grin and a smirk, asked if I would run down to Starbucks and bring him a cup of coffee. I couldn't believe it!

This was my grandmother's workplace of the 1950s! Women were considered no more than waitresses. And now it was happening to me. But, guess what, I marched down to the first floor and brought back his coffee. I even said, "Can I get anything for anyone else?"

That was stupid, I know, but I didn't know how to handle the situation. Obviously, there are some circumstances in which lower-level employees, both men and women, would be expected to get coffee for others, as a part of their jobs. But where the request is based not in job expectations but clearly reflects sexist bias and discrimination, as it did in this case, it shouldn't be tolerated.

Would a man have been asked to get the coffee? Probably. Would he have done so? Maybe. But this was different. Howard clearly chose the one woman among the several younger employees present.

If I had said, "Sorry, that's not my job," I suspect that I would've been labeled a troublemaker. And this was a guy with a lot of seniority, so I caved. Yes, sexism is alive and well in America. And sometimes I don't even know whether I'm a victim or perpetrator.

But I want to learn from this experience. The next time something like this happens, I want to be ready with a response that helps me establish boundaries between Clark and me.

Holy crap, that sounds so simple! But I have no idea what I could do.

I want to fully participate in leadership, being recognized, being included, being heard, and being respected. I know a lot of that is on me, but I don't want the extra roadblocks of old stereotypes getting in my way. I have too much to do.

Looking back through these three examples, I guess that the thread that connects all these incidents is my desire for "respect."

What you called "Just Plain Good Management" would seem to me to support the idea of respect, even compassion for others. In fact, I remember your saying, "Care about your people and let that caring show." Maybe I'm just confused. But the difference between the ideal that we talked about in class and the reality that I face sometimes at work is striking. I hope that our letters back and forth will help me sort out these issues.

I apologize for rambling so much, but maybe this will get us started. I'm curious about our letters and look forward to Mike's and your next one.

Kayla

3
LETTER FROM MIKE
September 12

Professor,

Thanks so much for including me in this project. I think it's great that I have a chance to exchange these letters with you and Kayla. As you said, this should be fun – and very helpful. Thanks for the opportunity.

Kayla sent me a copy of the letter she just sent to you and I'll follow that pattern by copying her on this letter. Kayla is a very bright young woman and someone I trust. I'll enjoy working with her.

At the end of your first letter, you suggested that Kayla and I begin our discussions by describing some personal experiences in our work, presumably some that are likely to shape our leadership.

I want to focus here on a couple of things that have been on my mind recently. The first has to do with what I guess we could call generational issues, the second with some more personal concerns.

Our last class discussion, the one on challenges facing young leaders, really got me thinking about the way age differences affect the way that my colleagues and I interact with each other at work. (As you know, I'm in my ninth year working in the financial area of a large corporation here in northern California.)

As I think back to my earlier days in the company, I certainly faced some generational issues – and, I guess, I still do. Maybe every generation coming into the workplace is subject to some teasing, even modest "hazing." However, as Kayla said, our generation has become a special target for those of preceding generations. People question our work ethic, our commitment to the organization, and our capacity for long-range thinking. They also assume that we are all the same, a kind of stereotyping that wouldn't be allowed in other kinds of comparisons.

10 Letter from Mike September 12

I imagine it's natural for people from older generations to question those who are younger. The two groups simply bring different experiences to their work, they communicate in different ways, and they don't have the same "style." They have different views of the world and reconciling their differences can be difficult.

I think the actual differences between the generations are pretty small. Our generation is probably more like other generations than we are different. Though age-wise I fall in the upper range of the so-called millennials, I don't really use that term. It conveys a stereotype I don't believe in. There's no question that some millennials are every bit as self-absorbed and dependent as our worst stereotype. But they don't represent all of us, and I get particularly upset when these outliers give the rest of us a bad name.

I also think senior managers often ground their opinion of our generation in slogans rather than facts. The judgments people make about many things are often close calls, and I think that's the case here. For example, some say that millennials are self-absorbed, maybe even narcissistic. But there's a thin line between self-absorption (bad) and the kind of confidence that is needed for leadership (good).

Saying someone has a short attention span or fleeting interests (bad) may just be evidence of what is really curiosity and broad interests (good). To say that millennials change jobs too quickly (bad) may be to say that the jobs they leave are not providing the development experiences they need (good). Like so many things, when people talk about age differences, the positives and negatives may be much less dramatic than they at first appear.

And, by the way, those above me in the organization, including many of those who are most critical of the younger ones, are not in a particularly good position to talk. They are often rigid and self-centered, not very creative or imaginative, and not really interested in their employees' growth and development. I remember we reviewed some research in class that made that point, and that has been my experience here in our company. Maybe in our letters we can examine what's expected of those heading today's organizations and make some suggestions about how those people might become more flexible and open to change. (These letters are confidential, right?)

That comment may be a good transition to some personal concerns I have when I think about my own leadership development. Kayla mentioned issues such as communication and commitment, etc., and, of course, we encounter the same problems in our organization. But I want to add to our list something about the way we experience our lives and our work "from the inside."

After being with my organization for some time, I understand the company's culture and, even though I am sometimes critical of that culture, I still work well with the people around me.

But questions about what it all means are the ones that bother me the most. These questions usually stay beneath the surface, but occasionally they become so pressing that I can't avoid sharing them with those around me, especially my wife or good friends. (Incidentally, my wife is very supportive, but I think she may be a little worried about me. Is my confusion normal?)

In any case, I don't want to seem overly dramatic, but I've been spending a lot of time recently trying to figure out who I am and where I'm going – and, most of all, what it means. I know these are huge philosophical questions, but they're also very personal and practical questions.

I would say that I am currently on a path of self-discovery. I know where I have been, but I want to figure out where I go now. I am really looking for who I am becoming and who my ideal self is. I am feeling compelled to move in a new direction at a time when most would say it doesn't make sense. Maybe I need a new way of looking at what I'm doing and what I'm feeling. It's hard for me to even talk about leadership without addressing some of these personal issues first.

One last note. After being contacted last week by a search firm, I applied for a position with a larger company in my field. The job would be in Los Angeles and I would have significantly more leadership responsibilities (and more money!). I'll keep you posted.

Well, having said that – more than I expected – I'll stop for now. I don't know that I answered your questions; in fact, I'm pretty sure I didn't answer many. But I imagine there will be time for that later. At least you get an idea of the concerns I'm dealing with.

I'm thinking this letter idea is very cool, and I hope that I can contribute as well as learn from you and Kayla over the coming months. Thanks for including me.

Mike

4

LETTER FROM BOB

October 2

Dear Kayla and Mike,

Your letters arrived within a couple of days of one another, so I'll try to respond to both. I really appreciate your openness in sharing things that are happening in your lives that relate to your current role in your organizations and your interest in leading in those settings and others.

Kayla, my friend Robert (yes, your CEO!) tells me that you are someone expected to move quickly into the leadership circle in his firm. You seem committed to that trajectory but remain concerned about some of the roadblocks that you will have to navigate in your leadership journey. Some are issues faced by anyone aspiring to a top-level position – learning the business, building a network of contacts and support throughout the company, and developing maturity and self-confidence – all aspects of preparing to move up. But, as you point out, there are some issues you face that are distinctly related to the conflict of generations in the workplace and some that reflect the role of women in contemporary organizations.

Mike, I was also taken with your words: "I am currently on a path of self-discovery. I know where I have been, but I want to figure out where I go now." You have been quite successful in your early corporate career, but you are uncertain as to your future life's calling. (As you will see, my use of the word calling is much broader than its use in a narrow vocational sense.)

In your uncertainty, I think you are joined by many of your contemporaries, including Kayla, who talked about her own "identity." You are poised to lead, but you want to be sure that your leadership is meaningful. You find excitement and fulfillment in your leadership at home, in your community, and at work, but you sometimes wonder "What does leading really mean in its broader sense – and what about leading would I find meaningful or significant?"

One approach to responding to this question is to reverse the question and to ask, "What is there inside me that would provide a meaningful reason for someone to follow?" To reach your greatest potential as a leader, you must acquire practical skills and develop personal qualities. But also, especially for your generation, you need to understand what it all means – to you and to others.

Leadership is not just about employing a certain set of skills but is a quality, a sense of being and becoming, that we carry with us every day. It's important for you as emerging leaders to explore that complex of qualities, commitments, and values that you hold inside and that are reflected in your behavior in the outside world. At the same time, you should reflect on the impact you are having on others, especially as your life and your leadership contribute to their search for meaning and significance.

In my experience, students talk in class about skills, but in more quiet, reflective settings, they are more concerned about how leadership affects the totality of their lives and the lives of others around them. Our late USC colleague Warren Bennis put it perfectly, as he often did, when he said, "The process of becoming a leader is similar, if not identical to, the process of becoming a fully integrated human being."

The two of you certainly raised that issue in your letters. Kayla, you hit the nail on the head in your analysis of what you had written. You focused on the importance of human relationships and the importance of respect and trust in those relationships. "Respect" is clearly something you desire in the workplace and something you should expect, even demand. And, Mike, the word "meaning" or the phrase "the search for meaning" jumped out from what you wrote.

In any case, the issues you both raised are consistent with what I hear from other young and emerging leaders. These are questions that you and others have, and they are connected to both what you need to do to become a leader and the personal experiences that you have along the way. But they also reflect some limitations that our current way of thinking about leadership places on us. More about that later.

Leading Through the Generations

But first let's talk about the conflicts between young employees and their more experienced colleagues that both of you described. You especially wondered why those should turn into battles. I think it was you, Kayla, who said "Why all the drama?" Certainly, there are differences among the generations in terms of culture, especially art and music, in terms of marriage and family structures, in terms of politics, and in terms of what constitutes meaningful human experience. But let's focus here on those related to our experiences in leadership in organizations. I want to offer two suggestions related to *leadership* as to why those differences might lead to conflict.

First, you have grown up in a digital world and are comfortable with the tools and devices of modern information technology; those more senior in the organization find this mystifying and in turn threatening to their continued control – as perhaps they should.

For centuries, even millennia, most people around the world lived relatively stable lives. Many were isolated by geography. Others were isolated by social and political restrictions. And all were isolated by the difficulty of communicating across long distances. But with the advent of modern travel, with the opening of boundaries to trade and cultural exchanges, and, of course, with the advances of modern information technology, societies became less stable and more "liquid" – that is, rigid institutional boundaries became more elastic and more penetrable. The constraints of space and time were at least partially lifted, and change became the norm.

Only a few years ago, we lived in a stable society punctuated by bursts of change. Today, we live in a rapidly changing society punctuated by moments of stability.

Nowhere has change been more dramatic than in the way we communicate with one another. In fewer than 30 years, we have gone from the world of faxes and landline phones (which, you may remember, in your childhood were called "telephones") to a world of smartphones, social media, virtual reality, and artificial intelligence.

At the same time, social media keeps you in touch with one another 24/7. The expansion of Facebook, LinkedIn, Twitter, Instagram, and so on has meant that your generation relies on very different media than those of previous generations. Consequently, to the extent that the medium is the message, you are speaking one language and your senior managers are speaking another – at least that's the way they perceive it.

Moreover, you are comfortable with a much more fast-moving society than the one that they grew up in. What they (or I) might think of as a situation of rapid change, you might perceive to be normal.

This disconnect leads many senior managers to be suspicious of your generation. People often fear those they don't understand, and they assume that the newbies are bent on wrestling control away from them. Though I don't see your generation as particularly interested in gaining power or control per se – indeed you seem to me more interested in autonomy and personal choice – certainly some perceive you as challenging their power. The differences in the rhythm of your generation and the mysterious language you speak have the unintended effect of creating chasms between generations.

In addition, as I mentioned earlier, there has been an important change in the way we view the world of work, a change your generation can take considerable credit for. Your expectations with respect to the quality of your work life and the rewards you seek are higher than ever before. But your generation also expects to find work that is meaningful and makes a difference. You are sensitive to finding jobs with purposes and values consistent with your own, and you are willing to move to seek more meaningful work.

With the insistence of your generation – though with a generous kick-start from ours – people have become more adamant about increasing autonomy in their work lives and elsewhere. Over the past decades, trust in government, trust in business, trust in the media, trust in unions, trust in religion have all declined dramatically, suggesting a widespread questioning of authority.

Slogans such as "Power to the People" and "Question Authority" are decades old, and even though they are dated, their message still rings true today: people just don't like to be told what to do. They don't like to be "managed," certainly not "bossed around." They especially don't want to be "bullied."

People today want to determine their own destiny. And this is already impacting the way we organize and the way we lead. But what your generation sees as a search for human meaning, for human connection but also autonomy, others see as a challenge to their authority. Their message is "there's work to be done, you've got a job, we pay you, get over it." Altogether, it makes for very tenuous relationships among the generations.

Second, while generations prior to yours have largely accepted the value of large organizations in our society and have in turn been willing to play "by the rules," you seem much more skeptical about today's organizations. You are more likely than previous generations to ask whether there are serious negative consequences of organizational work.

Some of Those Negatives

There is no question that large organizations, especially corporate and governmental organizations, have had a tremendous impact on our society. In many cases, that impact has been positive, but there are also ways in which it has been negative. Moreover, those we call leaders today provide powerful and not always helpful models for all of us as we go through our lives, in organizations or outside them. I'm thinking particularly of the way that power is displayed in organizations and in our society generally, the way that ethical behavior is prescribed for the organizational world and beyond, and the way those two get tangled up with one another. Let's explore a few of these ideas.

Surely our major leaders and their organizations can claim great material and technological advances over the decades. But our capacity to solve major problems of social and economic policy has improved only marginally, if at all. Moreover, many of our "advances" have caused political turmoil and social disruption. Many people have benefited from the work of large organizations, though many more have been left behind, even harmed.

For example, the old model of leadership and organization must be held at least partially responsible for damage to the environment, including climate change. In the corporate world, the primary measure of success has, of course, been the financial bottom line. Only recently have some corporate executives begun to talk about a second bottom line – the social impact of their work – or even a third – its environmental impact. What I am suggesting is not necessarily a reordering of these priorities (social and environmental impact first, fiscal performance second), though that's not a bad idea. Rather, I would say that a focus on the bottom line should never violate principles of fairness, equity, and sustainability.

Some will, of course, argue that self-interested behavior is the driver of economic performance, and that filtering for social and environmental values would damage the economy. But, of course, the fact that we have put economic interests first in the past has already caused serious damage, contributing to war, famine, massive poverty, climate change, and so on. We are surely in need of an alternative.

To that point, our current way of leading and organizing has helped create an incentive structure that has led to severe income inequality. The richest 1 percent of America's population holds just under 40 percent of the nation's wealth, almost twice as much as the bottom 90 percent. Lower- and middle-income Americans have seen their incomes remain relatively stagnant or even decline, while those at the top have benefited most from the economic recovery and tax "reform." Of course, a significant driver of income inequality over the past couple of decades has been the extraordinary compensation of corporate "super managers."

Inequality is damaging in many ways. Not only does it foster differences in health outcomes, the crime rate, and opportunities for upward mobility, but it encourages decreased productivity, reduced consumption, and drags on the economy. Again, some would say that inequality is the price of economic growth, but the evidence supports the opposite view. Even the International Monetary Fund has concluded that "lower net inequality is robustly correlated with faster and more durable growth."

Future organizations must be based on incentive structures that reward those who bring a clear sense of purpose and commitment to doing work that makes a positive difference in the world. If leadership is distributed throughout the organization, those willing to lead will do so based on what they may be able to accomplish as opposed to what they will acquire, what they will learn rather than what they will earn. Moreover, if leadership is separated from ego and ambition, leaders will be much less likely to make questionable ethical decisions based on the assumption of their infallibility. (More on this later.)

Finally, our personal lives have also been affected. Our lives have been improved with modern conveniences, but we also suffer from materialistic accumulation or "clutter." (As a so-called "early adopter" – aka "early dropper" – I certainly have my share of technological toys, such as my camera-equipped drone, taking up space on my office floor – in that case, after just one test flight/crash!)

Also, the past several generations have lived in what I once called "the shadow of organization." Our lives have been defined by our roles in organizations more than by other life pursuits. For example, when you begin a conversation with a stranger sitting next to you on an airplane, the first question is always "What do you do?" or "What business are you in?" It's not "What do you enjoy?" or "What are you seeking from life?" (Indeed, if a new seatmate asked you these questions, you'd probably ask to be reseated!)

Just as our work in organizations is characterized by efforts to be rational and objective, we often follow the same pattern outside work, defining relationships in terms of transactions or exchanges, confusing success with greed and accumulation, and equating status and morality. The result has been described as conformity, alienation, inauthenticity, stress, confusion, or simply exhaustion (depending on which decade you're talking about).

In these several ways, your generation is seen as departing from the previous generations' dependence on organizations as both providers of needed goods and services, and as models for human interaction, broadly defined. From your perspective, these issues may seem trivial. But from the perspective of other generations, these differences are absolutely critical – they are questions of *power* and questions of *identity*. To the extent that you are seen as challenging the power and identity of previous generations – whether you are actually doing so or not – red flags are raised with respect to your motives and intentions. You are seen as threatening. And, consequently, the debates and discussions can get quite intense.

So, let's give this discussion time to sink in. I'm really curious about what you think of when you say "leadership." Then you might discuss what you find most effective in learning about leadership in your day-to-day work. And we can continue our conversation about roadblocks to leadership. I think that will lead us in some interesting directions. I also think that we have not heard the last of these issues of power and identity. They will likely come back to haunt us later!

Yours,

Bob

P.S. By the way, please don't feel you have to call me "Professor" or "Dr. Denhardt." I got over that a long time ago. I'd prefer that you just call me "Bob," but I realize that doing so may feel awkward for you. If so, maybe you would be more comfortable using the form of address that my friend Lisa G. uses. She calls me "Dr. Bob." I like that.

5

LETTER FROM KAYLA

October 14

Dr. Bob,

What an interesting start to our conversations! It's helpful to at least get some hints as to where we might go. Thanks also for your comments on the experiences Mike and I are having in our companies. I see some similarities, but also some differences. That's good!

And Mike, thanks for your nice comments about our working together. I look forward to that as well.

Dr. Bob, I think your comments on the threat that we young folks pose to others in our organizations make a lot of sense. But they may also raise some new questions that I hope we can address, questions about who has power in organizations and how they use that power, as well as questions about what makes for ethical leadership. You mentioned that we will come back to these topics so, for now, I'll just look forward to the discussion.

You asked us to write more about how we think about leadership and about what has been most helpful in our learning leadership.

I don't have a quick and easy definition of leadership, but what comes first to mind is that leaders have a vision, a picture of what the future should be. And they should have well-tuned interpersonal skills. But that may not be enough. They may also need some other quality – maybe something like charisma – that attracts people to them and makes them want to follow. I haven't figured out what that "magic dust" is or where you get it. I guess no one else has either, but I bet it would sell for millions.

What I personally find most helpful in learning about leadership is some combination of reading books and articles on the topic, discussing leadership with others, watching others lead, and experimenting with leadership myself.

I have tried to learn from the experiences of those around me in the company, from our CEO, Robert, to the front-line people. (Oh, by the way, I didn't know you knew Robert, but I appreciate your passing on his comments. He is low-key and even-tempered, but he is also an enormously bright and talented guy. I really like him.)

I'm a people person and enjoy watching others at work, and especially in meetings. I guess people-watching is not among the leading leadership development exercises taught in the universities, but for me it works.

I see two or three people walking together and try to guess who is leading. At our companywide meetings, I try to spot the ambitious few who are positioning themselves to interact with the executive level folks. (It's amazing how easy it is to identify ambition from a distance.)

I like to read, and I like to study people through watching them at work, but I also need to make those ideas a part of me. I need to try them out in real life, and not just in the everyday routine of the office. This may sound funny, but I think I learn the most when I'm involved in situations that present new challenges to me. Maybe when things are shaken up, less structured, there are more spaces for learning.

Of course, we did some simulations in class that were meant to mirror leading in the real world, but, while they pointed out some good lessons, they remained a little artificial. I need to bring those lessons back to work and try them out in the office or with clients. I might talk with Robert about how I can gain some of those experiences early on.

In terms of roadblocks, I've already mentioned the different views people have about their work and about management, and I talked about sexism and discrimination. These are "outside" roadblocks, but there may be some that come from inside as well. Sometimes I may be my own worst enemy. I've never been a particularly shy person, but I find in my current setting that I'm somewhat hesitant to jump into things as quickly or forcefully as I might have before. I'm know I can do the work, but I seem to lack the self-confidence to lead.

That's never been a problem for me before. In high school, I was always active and involved in class activities and even edited the school yearbook. I was voted by my high-school senior class to be "The Most Likely to Appear on the Cover of *People Magazine*." Much the same through college. And my Facebook friends must number in the four figures by now. So where does this new questioning and self-doubt come from? Maybe I'm just not yet comfortable in my job, maybe I fear rejection more pointedly now that I'm in the "real world," maybe I don't really want to lead. I guess that's something we can discuss.

Well, I'll end for now. I hope this is helpful, and I'll be looking forward to your next letter.

Kayla

6
LETTER FROM MIKE
October 20

Bob

When I think of words like "lead," "leader," or "leadership," I frankly get very confused. There doesn't seem to be any consistency among these terms. Someone can hold a position of leadership, say, the head of a corporation, and yet not lead. You can even be the president of the United States, the presumed "Leader of the Free World," and still have people question your leadership abilities, including your competencies, your stability, and your moral compass. But you are still called a leader. I really think it's something that needs to be straightened out.

With respect to the question of where I have learned the most about leadership, the answer would be where I have just read something about leadership or talked about it in class and then immediately thereafter encountered it in my work – or vice versa. I read a lot. But reading by itself doesn't connect with me personally. I feel like I learn much more when I can connect my reading with my own experience.

You made a big deal in class about integrating theory and practice, and I guess that's what I'm talking about here. Situations in which there is a close connection between "theory and practice" seem to me to provide great opportunities for learning about leadership. What was it you said about action and reflection? Was it: "Action without reflection is blind; reflection without action is futile." I get that!

The other thing that occurs to me is that we often do exercises or study cases in class, but, as Kayla said, they are somebody else's reality, not mine. I can learn something from those experiences, but I'm more interested in my own perspectives and my own reactions than how somebody in 1982 acted. I understand that, even though what happened in 1982 is not going to happen to me in exactly that way, I can draw some general lessons from the case study that may apply. But how do you apply these lessons in the "real world," *my* real world.

Of course, almost everything that happens to us day-to-day at work or in class or in the grocery or at church is a real-life experience. And almost every one of those real-life experiences can tell us something about leadership, because they can tell us about ourselves. Learning about me is, I believe, a very important part of learning about leadership, maybe the most important part. I don't think we are lacking in opportunities to learn, but we may be failing to recognize some of them.

Certainly, you must be self-reflective and self-critical to learn the most from your experiences. You must recognize when you are learning and what you're learning. You must step back and think through exactly what was going on and understand your own reactions. And you must be willing to critique those parts of your own ideas and your own behavior that don't seem right. As you said before, we must start inside and build out.

Finally, you asked about some of the roadblocks we have encountered in advancing our leadership potential. I think I've already mentioned one, and that is not recognizing the opportunities we have to learn about leadership and not taking advantage of those situations that could be most helpful to us. If we're going to learn to lead, we must be open to any experience that will help shape us into more mature and confident leaders.

They say knowing yourself is the first step to leading others; surely continuously educating yourself is the second. But I also remember your saying in class something I thought was important – well, everything you said in the class was important! – but this was so important that I wrote it down. You said, "Learning to lead is about learning to learn. And learning to learn is about the whole person."

On that note, let me shift gears and tell you a bit about what's been happening with my negotiations in Los Angeles. (This really has been an opportunity for me to think through my management and leadership capabilities, as well as to think through the situations in which I would be comfortable and feel good about leading.) After I made a couple of trips to interview with the company, they decided to make me an offer – and a very good one at that!

While that was exciting and flattering, we just weren't sure whether this was the right move at the right time.

As you know, my wife Annie is a poet and would like to spend more time writing. Our current circumstances, with children and all, make that very difficult. Our first thought was that Los Angeles might provide a better locale for her, mainly because Los Angeles is such a center for creativity. But we began to recognize that there would be many adjustments we would have to make, and while I could help with some, many of the transition issues would fall to her.

We talked with family and friends about the move and they were extraordinarily helpful in focusing our attention on personal and emotional matters as opposed to simply the calculus of my salary here versus my salary there and my benefits here versus my benefits there. I even had a long talk with members of my hiking club as we sat around the campfire at the top of a mountain – well, a hill we had climbed. From that vantage point, I admit I could almost conjure up the lights of LA County – I think that's a song, isn't it? They were tempting, but so was the idea of being able to sit with this group of close friends by a campfire from time to time.

They say for people of our generation, making transitions is supposed to be easy. But our generation is also said to be very concerned with maintaining a high quality of life – and for Annie and me that means having friends and family close by.

I don't have to decide about the new job for another couple of weeks, so we will continue to think about this and talk with lots of different people. Of course, I'd appreciate your insights as well. One thing to consider is where this fits with my leadership aspirations and leadership journey, and I hope you can help with that. Let me know your thoughts.

Mike

7
LETTER FROM BOB
October 31

Dear Kayla and Mike,

Thanks to both of you for your thoughtful responses to my last letter.

Kayla, you commented on the high expectations of those above you in the organization, but also on your lack of confidence in the work you are doing. As you pointed out, you have every reason to feel positive about what's happening at work and about moving into a position where your leadership can make a difference. You did well in school, your early career has been marked by success and recognition, and it is clear your company is providing opportunities for you. Yet you may still be reluctant to lead.

In some ways, that surprises me because I see you as an extremely capable young woman, fully ready to take on any new challenge, and likely to rise quickly in the organization. You don't seem power hungry to me. You don't seem obsessed with promotion or more money. Instead, you seem to have taken to heart the challenge that was issued during our class and probably reinforced by your parents – that is, to seek a position in which you can lead with meaning and make a difference.

But I do understand what you are talking about and I know that your view is not unusual among women your age. I wonder if part of the issue – though certainly not the only factor – relates to the role of women in today's organizations. I imagine that, as you were growing up, you watched the struggles of women like your mother, and empathized with them. After all, that generation of women was told time after time that they couldn't do the job, that they didn't have what it took to lead, that they didn't "fit in."

Of course, over the long term, they demonstrated that they not only could lead, but that they could lead quite effectively. But the constant battle to establish that fact must have been wearing on them and, in turn, affected you and your generation.

Equally important, or maybe even more so, is the fact that you have already experienced some of the same struggles yourself. While many in the media proclaim the victories of women in breaking the glass ceiling, you realize that sexism is not dead. The old prejudices are still there, sometimes subtler, but often even more dramatic.

Your mother grew up with different experiences than her male counterparts, whether in school, in athletics, and in your work experiences. She was often shut out of opportunities to lead, and her capabilities in leading were often questioned, mostly by men, but even by some women. But you are experiencing many of these things yourself! The old prejudices may be dying ever so slowly, but they are still with us today.

Meanwhile, men like your father seemed to move easily and naturally into higher positions. As much as they might be churning inside, and as much as they might have doubted their expertise, they appeared confident and capable. You might be surprised to learn that they (we) were often filled with self-doubt as well.

I remember the story of a newly hired city manager who was moving into his new house in the community. As he was trying to get settled, he accidentally pulled the handle off his refrigerator. Immediately, he broke down into tears. His wife told him, "It's just a refrigerator handle." He answered, "No. It's not the refrigerator. I just don't know if I can do the job."

(This story resonates with me because, while I didn't break a refrigerator door, when I went to my very first class session as a teacher, I had no idea what I was doing and I was scared to death. And if that wasn't enough, I soon learned that the university president's daughter was in my class!)

Vulnerability is not the exclusive property of women, and self-confidence is not the exclusive property of men, but I can certainly understand how you might perceive that to be the case. The cultural expectations surrounding men and women in the workplace remain both strong and biased, something we need to change.

We should address the leadership challenges of women in the workplace, but first, I'd like to hear a little bit more about what you're thinking and experiencing. I'd also like to learn more about what you're confronting with respect to the question of power in organizations and the role of power in leadership.

And, Mike, I appreciated your letter telling me of your negotiations on a possible career move. I think you would enjoy being in Los Angeles – I've certainly found it an attractive "home away from home." There's a special energy there, as well as a diversity of cultures and creatives. But you surely will find the cost of living, especially housing, to be much higher. And, of course, there's that traffic thing!

For this reason, I think you are correct to have conversations not only with people you know professionally at work but also with relatives and friends (not that relatives and friends are mutually exclusive!). They will help you balance your professional interests with your personal and family interests. And if some of those conversations lead you to a hilltop and a campfire all the better. What a nice image!

The earlier part of your letter raised many questions that I want to try to address, questions about what constitutes leadership and, importantly, questions about how the way in which we define leadership opens or closes certain doors for us. I am convinced that the way we define the broad concepts like leadership has consequences for our actions, opening some opportunities for us, blocking others.

Though there may be one or two words that we consider key to leadership, more likely, leadership brings up several different images, including recollections of our experiences in leading, expectations of our culture with respect to leadership, and our own capacity for and commitment to the process of leading. So, what we're doing here is not just an exercise in lexicography; it is a matter of establishing both boundaries and possibilities for action.

Leadership Energizes

Leadership is confusing for several reasons. As Kayla said, when people try to define leadership, the first word that usually comes to mind is vision. We think of leaders as being distinguished from others by their having a vision, a convincing idea about where the group or organization should go. But simply holding a vision without mobilizing action isn't leadership. Indeed, it's more likely to be called "fantasy."

In any case, vision is rarely the property of any one individual. The problems we face are much too complex for one person to be able to define a vision. Leadership is not merely about an individual having a vision. There must be something that engages the group, that causes it to act.

It's also confusing that we use the terms "leader" and "leadership" to describe positions in a group or organization. As Mike pointed out, the CEO is called the "leader of the Corporation," and the President of the United States is called the "leader of the free world." But we know that often these "leaders" don't lead effectively. They may not even lead at all.

Just holding an office titled "leader" is not the same as leading. The officeholder may lead, just as others may lead, but it's not the position someone holds that makes that person a leader. It's what they can do. Yet our culture has defined leadership to essentially mean the same thing as the "chief executive."

We also tend to associate leaders with power. But power is not the same as leadership. In fact, many would say that power is the opposite of leadership – if you must resort to power, you are not really leading. Certainly, those with power can do good things (or bad things). But just the fact they hold power doesn't make them leaders. Power is not essential to leadership and, especially in the long run, can be detrimental. It can and often does backfire. And as we will see, it can contribute to damaged relationships and miscommunication within groups and organizations – but we'll come back to that later.

Leadership then is not just having a vision, nor is it simply high-level management. It is not holding an office, having a title, or exercising power. So, what do we mean by saying that someone is leading or exercising leadership?

We know that leadership occurs in many places: children lead their classmates, while adults lead in families, churches, communities, and businesses. But how can we describe the act of leading so that it applies to all these settings? What do people do when they lead?

I have given up trying to provide a dictionary type definition of leadership. But another way to approach defining something is to describe the meaning and significance that it carries. It's in that sense that I have proposed a 36-word academic description of leading; I also have a one-word practical definition.

Let's start with the academic version: *Leading occurs when one or more individuals stimulate other members of a group or organization to more clearly recognize the manifest and latent needs, desires, and potentialities that they share and to work toward their fulfillment.* In this sense, leadership doesn't involve a potential leader imposing his or her ideas or vision on a group. To the contrary, leadership involves a continued dialogue between the leader (or leaders) and the group. In this view, leadership is a process that must involve many people. It's all about relationships.

The active verb in my definition is, of course, "stimulate." It is not "control," it is not "direct," and it is not even "influence." Leading involves helping others to clarify what's currently happening in the group or organization, its manifest values and commitments, its typical patterns of action, and its relation to its environment. Then the leader helps others to recognize their shared "needs, desires, and potentialities," some of which may be consciously held, but many of which will be hidden beneath the surface of the group's activities and even beneath the surface of individual consciousness. Leading, then, involves stimulating the group to identify new possibilities for action that may have been hiding nearby all along.

The one who leads, however, is decidedly not just a passive participant in this process. Rather, a leader raises the aspirations of the group by providing creative insights, finding new ways of putting the puzzle together, and exploring new patterns of meaningful action. These new patterns, brought forth in a group process then articulated by the leader, are so powerful that they compel the group to act. In this respect, the act of leading involves pulling ideas from the group and its environment, identifying, contributing to, and then articulating a new way of thinking about the group's direction, and mobilizing action in that direction.

Of course, this approach implies that it would be better for us to focus on "acts of leading" rather than trying to define a leader. As opposed to a leader being someone who holds a particular office or position, I would say that the leader is someone who leads. That is, the leader is someone who engages others, helps them identify their greatest potential, and moves them to act.

With this definition, leading can occur on the playground or in the boardroom. It can occur in the family or in the agency or in the corporation. The "act of leading" is fundamentally the same in all these settings. Our focus in understanding and practicing leadership should be first on identifying acts of leading. In turn, we can call someone who engages in acts of leading a "leader."

Though my academic side likes the precision of the 36-word definition of leading, I suspect you are more likely to remember my one-word characterization of leadership: *leadership "energizes."* I think that the essence of leading is the leader's capacity to energize others. Whenever a group, organization, community, or society has been energized, I would say that an act of leadership has just occurred.

Think about how things happen in small groups or teams. Typically, the group will come together, and the conversation will drift back and forth for a while, skipping across various topics in a somewhat random fashion. Then, someone will say something that people find compelling, and the conversation will take off. The group has been energized. I would say that when this happens an act of leading (or leadership) has just occurred. Now, that act of leadership may not have been the act of a formal leader. In fact, in many groups like this there is no formal leader. But the one who energizes the group has exercised leadership.

You know the feeling of meeting or spending time with someone and coming to recognize that he or she has a depth of character and enthusiasm that you find contagious – you feel energized by that person. It's this exchange of energy that is the essence of leading, and it is something that can happen almost anywhere – from the playground to the boardroom.

Why use the word energize? It is because we are made up of energy, and we connect with each other through exchanges of energy, especially social and emotional energy. Over the past several decades, of course, the term "emotional intelligence" has emerged to describe someone who has a special sensitivity to and awareness of the emotional character of others, and who can connect with that emotional energy in building positive relationships. This is clearly a part of what we're talking about here. But there's more involved, as we will see.

You may properly question whether a definition of leadership deserves this much attention. However, when placed against the more familiar use of leadership as someone holding the top office in a group or organization, there is a very significant difference. I consider this a key point: *to define leadership as a position, specifically a top management position, locks us into a particular set of values and practices. And typically, that means adhering to an old model of leadership in organizations based on power and control.* As we will see, considering leadership as energizing, as tapping emotional energy, will allow us to consider new ways of leading based on empathy, caring, compassion, and love.

Leading on the Playground

This new way of talking about leading allows us to examine leadership in many different contexts. We can see acts of leading in families, in work groups, in churches, in politics and in many other settings. We can see a person leading, that is, engaging in acts of leadership, in many different places.

How about the experience of a little girl on the playground? Let's call her Mari. As are most of her classmates in the first grade, Mari is active and energetic and enjoys life. She has developed some academic skills, but also some basic social skills – and she demonstrates those skills daily. She is always near but not at the front of the line in the cafeteria, she raises her hand in class a little more often than most of her classmates, and the teacher occasionally asks her to play special roles, such as greeting visitors on behalf of the class. Mari has many friends in the class, and her friendships cut across ethnicities, backgrounds, and interests.

In the lunchroom, during breaks, and after school, Mari talks with her classmates and, more than others, she listens. She has a special capacity to understand her classmates' stories and ideas, what they like and what they don't, and she stores that information (albeit unconsciously) in a way that it can easily be recalled. She is also active in conversations, often suggesting new twists and turns that lead to both laughter and new ideas.

Today on the playground, a large group of children is standing near the back wall. Mari almost instinctively shouts, "Let's run!" and starts running around the perimeter of the playground. Nearly everyone in the group starts following her in a made-up running game that starts simply but takes on variations, such as students skipping or waving their arms as if they are flying. Mari has no control over what the group does, but she acts in a way that energizes the group, and when she suggests running, it is just the right suggestion. It energizes her classmates, and they follow in the game. Mari is a leader.

What do we learn from this example? One thing is that you don't have to be an executive in a corporation or government agency to lead. People throughout society lead and lead effectively, as Mari did.

But we also learn that leading sometimes appears to be the act of an individual, but that what has really happened is that the leader and the group have engaged in an often extended, complex, and convoluted process of relationship building and mutual understanding.

Mari, of course, would not have used words such as "relationship building and mutual understanding" to describe what she was doing. She would be more likely to say she just enjoyed asking questions and learning what other people thought. But this quiet questioning and exploration of the ideas of others is essential to the act of leading. The fact that it is informal, not done through structured meetings or "focus groups," does not change the basic premise, that the leader must work with the group to identify and then articulate its potential.

I should also note that Mari was sensitive, perhaps intuitively sensitive, but sensitive nonetheless to including a wide variety of her classmates in these discussions. You could almost call this "democratic inquiry," as it involves eliciting information and ideas "of the people, by the people, and for the people," all the people.

Again, why is this reconstruction of what leadership is all about, important? Because a new definition of leadership may enable us to think outside the proverbial box – and, for that matter, to act outside the proverbial box.

I'm hoping we can go into this further as our correspondence continues, but for now I'll close this letter, and write another in a couple of days. I already have some thoughts about that next letter, and I'd suggest that you wait to respond until you have seen both.

For now, good evening!

Yours,

Bob

8
LETTER FROM BOB
November 5

Dear Kayla and Mike

Let's continue to think about what leading means. We said that leaders stimulate, inspire, and articulate the group's potential and direction. They energize the group and its members. But they do so typically within the context of an interaction between the leader and the group. Understanding that interaction is crucial to understanding leadership.

In some cases, such as Mari's, it is very subtle, though I would say that the key to Mari's leadership was her constant attention to the group and her gently helping the group identify possibilities for action. This interaction, which is essential to the process of leadership, results in a defining moment in which the group recognizes that an act of leading has occurred and they begin to follow. This is the instant when people are energized. This is the "leadership moment."

In my view, this moment is critical to leadership; it is the moment in which leaders gain followers. Getting to this moment, however, is far from simple. Let's try to understand the basics first, then add more texture and complexity. What is it specifically that happens that culminates in the leadership moment? How can you, as a potential leader make the connection that enables you to energize potential followers?

First, the leadership process begins with your interaction with others, in most cases participants in a group or organization. You must engage in a sustained conversation that offers a free and open exchange of ideas about the group and its possible futures. This conversation can be quite informal or it can be more structured. It can involve one meeting, or more likely, it will involve a series of conversations. These may range from talks with individuals in the elevator or the parking lot to more formal retreats or planning sessions. But, in any case, this conversation is essential to the leadership process. From this exchange, the leader will identify the ideas and aspirations that are most important to the group and translate those elements into clear and compelling statements of purpose and direction.

Second, this interaction will only occur if the group grants you "standing" – that is, the group considers you to have sufficient knowledge, skill, or status that they will engage in the conversation with you. You can achieve standing by the position you are currently in, by your experience and reputation, by who introduces you to the group, by your initial persuasiveness, or in other ways. You maintain standing by proving credible, trustworthy, ethical, and so on.

Third, you engage in a sequence of actions to energize the group and maintain that energy over time. There are things you can do to increase the odds of energizing the group, and I'll put them in terms of actions that you as a potential leader must undertake. (Note that these five actions will typically move in this order, but there may be places where the order changes – and that's okay.)

1) Engage and inquire – Talk with everyone you can inside and outside the group or organization, current or potential. Read everything you can about the group or organization. Learn the organization inside and out. More importantly, learn the people, and begin to build genuine human relationships.
2) Identify Patterns – Seek out patterns among the many and often divergent views about the organization that you encounter. (Pattern recognition is the ability to see order in a chaotic environment – again, more on that later.) What are the recurring themes? What are the aspirations? What are the untapped resources? At some point you will likely add your own voice to the conversation, asking questions and providing insights that may not have come up before. You are not just taking in information. You are fully participating in a dialogue in which you and members of the group are both active and contributing.
3) Articulate the Purpose – Before even thinking the word "vision," articulate the purpose of the group or organization. Why does it exist? Based on your understanding of the history and potential of the group, put its purpose into words. Be sure to state it in a way that shows clearly why being involved in the group will be a significant and meaningful experience, one that will make a real contribution. Turn potential into purpose, and recognize that purpose – why we exist – is a compelling force for both individuals and groups and organizations.
4) Tell the Story – Having established the purpose of the group or organization, the next step is to clarify its future direction. Put this in terms of a story that points to the future, that connects the legacy of the organization to its future. Mark the path it will take. A few arrows or examples planted here and there will help focus the direction. Then tell the story, retell the story, and tell it again, until you're sick of it. Then tell it again. And tell it with energy and enthusiasm, caring and compassion, insight and emotion. The narrative and

the way you communicate it are key to energizing the group. If you succeed, you will see the sparks of energy and engagement. You will see commitment and action.

5) Align and Evaluate – In my view, leaders don't force action, they trigger action. You should discuss how organizational practices and actions are consistent with or differ from the narrative you've created. Moreover, people will judge the narrative not only by what you say, but also by what you do, maybe even more so. Realize the potency of your own actions. Every little statement or off-hand comment you make needs to be consistent with the "big picture," a part of the overall mosaic that you are putting together. Also, make sure you walk the talk, practice what you preach. People will watch you as well as listen to you – be your own best model. Finally, reflect on what has happened to you and to the group. What's the significance of what has happened? How does it advance the group's purpose? Most importantly, what does it mean – to you and to others?

Remember, most of all, that working through this sequence of actions is not the end of the process – quite the contrary. The dialogue must continue, and the narrative must be framed and reframed to meet evolving circumstances, within the group and in the larger society. Your work, the work of leading, is just beginning.

Movement over Time

How can the energizing effect of leadership be sustained over time? The quick answer is that the pattern of achieving standing then engaging in dialogue to reach a compelling story continues indefinitely. The longer answer needs to address how this occurs: what helps, and what gets in the way?

Interestingly, much of the mainstream literature on leadership deals with exactly these questions, though not in the way you might think. The traditional trait theories of leadership, for example, are not really theories of leadership per se. But, using our terminology, they are about maintaining standing.

The trait theories were largely based on surveys of what people saw as the most desired traits or characteristics of their leaders. As a school of leadership they failed, because the desired traits don't by themselves constitute the basis for leadership. For example, people want leaders who are (or at least appear to be) credible, honest, trustworthy, communicative, and the like. But being credible, for example, doesn't necessarily energize a group nor cause people to follow.

On the other hand, since these theories are based on the views of followers about their leaders, they constitute a good source of advice for those wishing to develop or maintain standing. To do so, you must meet the expectations of members of the group or organization as to what constitutes leadership. You must exhibit the traits that followers find most appealing.

Similarly, much of what falls into the behavioral approach to leadership is helpful in the continuing dialogue between the leader (you) and the group. There are many behavioral skills (delegation, for example) that are only marginally relevant to the process of leading, though they may be helpful in management. On the other hand, techniques such as active listening can obviously contribute to understanding how you can engage the group more effectively. Developing your "people" skills, especially those related to communications, is a necessary (though, as we will see, not sufficient) foundation for leading.

What about getting the work done? What about planning? What about productivity? These are key points, because your standing and engagement with the group are often shaped by the results that the organization is achieving.

While we have pointed out that simply holding a high-level position does not make someone a leader, often leaders will find themselves in a high-level position. If this is the case, then your success in *managing* the organization will have a profound effect on the group's perception of you. A record of success will make it easier for you to maintain the attention of organizational members, what we have called "standing."

I want to draw a sharp distinction between getting the job done and leading. Most of getting the job done is a management or executive function. This is where planning and productivity (and related concepts) are so important. But these elements are not leadership. Leadership as energizing may contribute to motivation and engagement by calling forth the best impulses of members of the group or organization. But the basics of management, including executive management – those activities related to planning, productivity, and so on – are not about leading. They are about execution.

You can both lead and manage, and while the two activities are different, they can be mutually reinforcing. Some executives are better at leading than managing; others are better at managing than leading. You can manage effectively and still not lead, or you can lead effectively and still not get results. You can fail at both or you can succeed at both. (I hope that's where you fit in!)

But remember, management, including executive management, is about execution. Leadership is about energizing.

The primary responsibility of the leader over time is "tending the narrative" – that is, maintaining standing, continuing the dialogue, evolving the group's core purpose and direction, and keeping a close watch on events swirling around the organization and affecting its interests and intent. You, more than others, must be able to grasp emerging social, cultural, political, and economic trends and understand their implications for the group's future. Your insight and awareness will significantly affect the group's evolving story, as they should.

This brings to mind the leader's role in organizational change. Leaders certainly help set a tone for change and stimulate action, but much of what is involved in the change process is actually the management of change. An executive team is likely responsible for identifying the specific changes that are desired, whether financial or cultural, as well as settling on an approach to change (restructuring or reorganization, organizational development, appreciative inquiry, etc.). Managers are also likely to be involved in measuring and evaluating the success of the change effort. But the work of the leader is to engage the group and to articulate a narrative that points to a new direction, and to connect with the organization's members in a way that energizes them in pursuit of that direction. Let's dig just a little deeper into this.

Notes on Change

Change inevitably involves the ideas and commitments that people hold dear based on reason, but also based on faith and conviction. Change involves moving away from the past and the present, both of which are at least comfortable in their familiarity. For this reason, change is almost always accompanied by emotional turmoil. Change is hard for most people, and it's hard because people are emotionally attached to their values.

Consequently, when people consider possible changes in their work or their organizations, they bring with them certain deep-seated, almost primal fears. There is the fear of the unknown, of ambiguity, and uncertainty. There is the fear of failure, of not being up to the challenges the future will bring. There is the fear of abandonment, of being stranded and alone. And there is the fear of losing control, of straying from our comfort zone.

The leader provides the assurance that the group needs to face the future. The leader is the one who says, "It's OK. We'll be fine. What we're doing is the right thing." The leader relieves the followers from the sense of loss or the guilt they might otherwise feel in moving away from long-standing patterns and preferences.

Organizational change is often seen as part of the process of rational planning. But there are also extremely important emotional and intuitive components involved in organizational change. Indeed, successful change efforts are attentive to both aspects – the rational and the intuitive, the logical and the emotional. Preserving that balance is your responsibility as a leader, and in our current society, which leans toward the rational, that often means giving voice to the intuitive and emotional.

In any case, through careful listening and measured communications, through articulating a new direction in a meaningful way, you can evoke a sense of commitment, even urgency to the change process. This is the act of leading.

Another Example

Let me share with you the story of Martin Cooper, president of the flagship public university in a Midwestern state. Cooper was selected for this position after a long search process by the Board of Regents, largely based on his experience as provost of a similar school in a nearby state. But Cooper had several advantages coming in: he was a native of the state; and while he didn't go to the university himself, he had many friends who did; he followed developments at the school over the years; and he had a good understanding of its history and traditions.

In the interview process, the board asked Cooper about his "vision" for the university, and he responded with an eloquent statement about the university's challenges and opportunities, based on his familiarity with the university and the "homework" he had done prior to the interview. His answer was also informed by his many previous conversations with friends, with members of the search committee, with individual board members, with faculty and staff who had called him (even another candidate for the position), and with members of the press, who were, it seemed, constantly at his side.

In his statement, Cooper emphasized the purpose of the university – to build the intellectual, social, and economic capacities of a new generation so that they might contribute to the continued growth and development of the state and its communities. This was not just Cooper's invention but a statement he had mentally drafted based on his talks with the many people he visited leading up to the board interview. He sketched out some basic ideas about the direction the university should take in the future.

But Cooper also maintained that the process of defining the future of the university rested, not only in his hands, but in the hands of members of the board, faculty, staff, students at the university, parents, alums, employers, political leaders, and other members of the community. He described the process of building the future of the university as one involving a wide range of people and interests, something he had already been doing prior to his interview.

Cooper was selected as chief executive of the university by the board, and that gave him further "standing" to engage the faculty, staff, students, alums, and others. But that didn't by itself make him a leader. The leadership moment remained.

As president, Cooper continued his practice of communicating with all groups. He spoke to anyone who would come and share their ideas with him. But even more than speaking, he listened. His schedule was unrelenting – meeting after meeting after meeting. Again, his appointment by the board gave him standing to engage the community, but his way of questioning, listening, and only then speaking, built confidence in those with whom he engaged.

After about six months into the job, Cooper gave a "State of the University" speech in which he articulated the purpose and direction of the university. His words hit home with those in the audience, as well as with those who read newspaper accounts or saw parts of the speech on television or on the university website. There was a decidedly positive reaction. This was the leadership moment.

But that moment was only the beginning. Cooper relied on the provost and other administrative officers of the university to keep the place running while he maintained his grueling schedule of meetings. In all cases, he opened with a restatement of the purpose and direction of the university that he had articulated in his speech, but he resisted the temptation to control the conversation and, instead, invited even greater levels of involvement in the work of the university (always, however, ending with a pitch for gifts and endowments!).

Throughout his tenure, Cooper remained humble and generous, recognizing that his telling of the university's story and its future was really the composition of many ideas and conversations that he had been able to shape and articulate, so they made sense to the broad community. Through trust and engagement, he maintained "standing." And other leadership moments followed.

Twelve years later, Cooper is a revered figure at the university and in the state. People say they would follow him anywhere. Just like Mari, Cooper is a leader.

Yours,

Bob

9
LETTER FROM KAYLA
November 10

Dr. Bob

I read through your last two letters several times, and I think I understand your "characterization" of leadership. But it's so different from the way we define leadership around here. When I think of moving to a leadership position, I think of moving up the ladder to a top-level slot (with a nice office!). That's the way we talk about leadership positions in our world.

You pointed out, however, that leadership is not just a matter of executive position but can happen anywhere. (I like your example of the playground!) The reverse also seems true. As Mike said, just because you're holding an executive position, you may not lead at all. I guess it clarifies things for me if I refer to those top positions as executive positions, rather than leadership positions.

I was listening to the news yesterday and the reporter said, "X Corporation has never had a woman leader." I think they meant they had never had a woman CEO. Surely they have had women lead from other positions – middle-management, staff positions, and everywhere else through the organization. I think this would be consistent with what you are saying. Right?

I understand your new definition of leadership, but I'm not completely sure I understand what difference it makes. Why would we need to redefine leadership? How would an organization change if we separated leaders from positions? And how would things be different if we cut the ties between leadership and power – which I'm not even sure we can do anyway. But I'm betting this is something that you're setting us up for! I'm willing to wait a while!

I would, however, like a little more explanation of the term "energy." The phrase, "leadership energizes," sounds right to me, but could you say more about what that really means? It sounds like you are again talking about drawing from one's own personal resources and capabilities to affect others, that "leader within" idea. I think I get it, but if you could add some language on energy, that would be very helpful to me.

Kayla

10
LETTER FROM MIKE
November 20

Bob

No developments on the job in Los Angeles. I hope I'll have something to report to you soon. Still struggling back and forth.

For now, I want to ask some questions about the "leadership moment." What you seem to be saying is that leadership, or leading, is not the act of an individual. Instead, leadership involves a relationship between the potential leader and the group. In that process, the leader mostly listens carefully to what the group is saying about the past, present, and future, and, along the way, provides ideas and comments that may somewhat reshape the narrative of the group. The leader then looks for patterns in what different groups say, and puts these together in a way that resonates with as many in the group as possible. In a sense, this becomes the vision of the organization, though you hesitate to call it "vision."

I hope I'm summarizing this in a reasonable way. Assuming I am, let me ask a couple of questions. First, I can see how this ties back to the "leadership energizes" definition. In neither case is the leader directing, imposing, or controlling. But that flies in the face of so much leadership literature and practice that I wonder if it's underplaying the role of the leader. Shouldn't the leader have more input into the definition of the narrative than simply reacting? And what is it that leaders do that energizes the group? Just listening to the group doesn't seem quite enough: what initiates the transfer of energy?

Second, what happens if the leader articulates the vision, but people don't accept it? Is there a fallback position for the leader, for example, to assert power?

Third, this seems such a long way from the traditional way of thinking about leadership in organizations, that I think you would have a hard time selling people on this new definition, at least with its fullest implications. I don't doubt that people would agree with the "energizing" part – though I would really like to see this fleshed out a bit – but they might disagree on what energizes, even arguing that power is sometimes necessary to energize.

Finally, there is simply the question of how you move from one interpretation of leadership to another, or from one way of leading to another. Even if we buy your definition of leadership and the way that it's implemented in the leadership moment, how does that view fare in a world that's constructed in far different ways? How might we bring about change in this direction?

I hope I'm not overstepping my boundaries in raising these questions, but you said you wanted critique. I hope you were serious about that.

Mike

11
LETTER FROM BOB
December 10

Dear Kayla and Mike,

I really enjoyed both your letters and appreciate the fact that you are willing to question some of these ideas. (Mike, you didn't overstep boundaries at all. Neither of you did.)

Both of you focused on my use of the term "energizing" as a key to understanding leadership. You asked for more detail about how leaders energize.

You also seemed concerned that the leader, in my description, is far too passive. The traditional view of leadership, as Mike pointed out, sees the leader as the most active person in the relationship. That's not necessarily the case in this new view. You also asked, given this understanding of the leader's role, how we could bring about change in the organizations we lead.

I'll elaborate on the question of energy in just a moment, and I'll discuss change later in a separate letter. Let me begin with whether my description of the leader's role makes the leader seem a passive actor. Does the leader just sit back and wait for the group to act?

No, I don't think so. The potential leader, in my view, does much more than listen to what the group or groups are saying. Rather the leader helps the group construct a narrative from the many disparate voices that enter the conversation. This can involve adding new material to the conversation, reshaping language so that different viewpoints are clarified and brought together, adding creative insight to the evolving narrative, negotiating positions taken by different groups, recognizing and accentuating recurring patterns in the discussion, and articulating the purpose in a way that stimulates members of the group to act.

The role of the leader in this process is a delicate one. On one hand, the leader needs to sit back and listen, not dominating the conversation in a way, but facilitating a good discussion. On the other hand, the potential leader must to some extent shape the conversation by adding new ideas and suggestions along the way. Again, importantly, what I'm calling a conversation or dialogue is not just one major meeting or two. It is a series of engagements of all types, some planned, some unplanned, some brief, some lengthy, some just conversations in the hallway.

It's also important to point out that although the dialogue we're discussing here is an exchange of ideas on the intellectual level, it also carries an emotional component. The potential leader must gauge the emotional power of the group's commitment to the organization and its purpose, as well as their ideas about where they might go next. Ultimately, the leader must touch people emotionally in a way that energizes them and causes them to act.

In this process, the most effective leader will also engage in continued self-reflection and self-critique, understanding and reframing his or her own ideas and values in a way that takes the group and its surrounding culture into account. Such work, work on the inside, is often the hardest work that the leader undertakes. The best contemporary leaders seem to understand, at least intuitively, the importance of this inner work and engage in it daily. In my view, this work is not just an add-on, but is absolutely central to the process of leading.

This way of leading is hard work, perhaps even harder than the work of the traditional leader, who can rely on power and directive to achieve coordination. The potential leader, in this view, has to shape a message so compelling that people will be moved to act. The energy that's transferred between the leader and the group is an energy generated by minds in conflict moving toward resolution. That's what human energy has always been about. All that we are doing here is applying that same notion to leadership.

What about Energy?

As I see it, the interplay of human energy is essential to human relationships. There are waves of energy that pulse through our bodies and connect us to one another, primarily through the emotions. These waves are reflected in many ways – through the physical rhythms of our heartbeats and our walking, through similar rhythmic patterns in groups and organizations, and through their capacity to shape space and time as a backdrop for leadership.

Let's look at this a little more closely. In my view, there are three aspects of energy that are important to leadership. The first is personal energy – the character and commitment that the individual who would lead brings to the leadership experience. The second is social energy – the flow of energy between and among people that ultimately moves them to become active in pursuit of mutual goals. I think that the flow of social energy is mostly stimulated by feelings and emotions; this is what causes the energizing effect of leadership. The third is moral energy, including moral imagination – the capacity to recognize the various possibilities for acting in a given situation and assessing the moral consequences of those alternatives.

Personal Energy

Let's think first about personal energy because much of what leaders do can be understood in terms of their transmitting energy to others.

Leaders are known for their action in the practical world, but they have to build a solid foundation of inner strength. They draw on the outer world for both insight and inspiration before acting, but ultimately, it's what's inside that really counts. Before acting, leaders must dig deep into their own consciousness and explore personal values to draw forth a new interpretation, a new formulation, a new twist on the way people have been viewing the world.

Almost paradoxically, it's only through this personal immersion that leaders can articulate the purpose and direction of the group. Your leadership will require you to explore and reveal the depths of your inner life, often in a very public way. Along with psychologist George Hagman, I would say that leadership, like art, does not merely capture how we feel: "It articulates who we are, a living person with an inner life with its rhythms and connections, crises and breaks, complexity and richness."

Certainly, there is a force or energy that lies within each of us. It is described differently in different traditions. Some call it "character"; some call it "consciousness"; some call it "soul." But in all cases, that personal energy constitutes a deep-seated self-understanding, a repository of caring and compassion, and a wellspring of creative action.

Personal energy can be expressed in many ways. For the leader, energy is expressed in self-confidence and self-esteem, both of which are necessary to negotiate times of risk and vulnerability. As a leader, your work will be under constant scrutiny and examination, a subject of endless discussion in the group or organization (as well as outside). Consequently, there is risk involved in every statement or proposal you make. To live in such an environment requires considerable self-confidence (though you must be careful not to allow self-confidence to turn into excessive ego).

Energy is also manifest in persistence and discipline, both of which are necessary to sustain a group or organization. Leadership can, of course, occur in a moment then drift away. And that's OK. But most leaders hope to sustain their contribution to the group or organization over time. For this, you need persistence and discipline.

Energy also expresses engagement, the capacity to interact with many people in many different circumstances. The leadership moment, as we saw with Mari and Cooper, is always preceded by a period of engagement. As a leader, you must be ready to listen to anyone at any time. You never know when even a brief conversation might yield an insight that would help in important ways to shape the group's direction.

Energy is also manifest in resilience, a capacity to bounce back or even thrive in the face of adversity. Resilience is especially necessary in order for you not only to tolerate change but to thrive under changing circumstances. Today's leaders need to expect the unexpected and when it arrives, to be able to adapt and to improvise.

As my colleague Rick says, "You have to learn to be comfortable with the uncomfortable." You have to understand and adapt to changes that may cause discomfort. And, as I have said, "You have to learn to be uncomfortable with the comfortable." If you are getting too comfortable, that probably means others are passing you by. You need to be ready to change.

Paradoxically, personal energy is also manifest in patience and tolerance. Until the future arrives, you must be able to deal with a great deal of uncertainty and ambiguity. While the adept leader can position the group or organization to take advantage of opportunities that the environment may present, there's often no way of knowing when or how those opportunities will present themselves. In the meantime, you need to remain relaxed but vigilant, ready to act when the time arrives.

Similarly, in times of turbulence (which means most of the time), you can serve the group well by modeling a sense of calm and tranquility. While moving quickly and with agility, you and your group must avoid acting out of panic. Undue stress makes communications among group members strained, and clouds both individual and group decision-making. The leader who projects a sense of self-control and relaxation under pressure can help restore a sense of calm and steadiness in the group as a whole. Note that "calm" is not the opposite of "energetic." You can be calm while at the same time being bold and forceful. Calmness projects its own energy, often with positive results. Calm is better thought of as the opposite of "out of control," something managers and leaders are all too often.

Finally, with respect to personal energy, realize that sheer intellectual capacity is important, but it may often be less important for your leadership than emotional agility – the capacity to connect with others in human, not mechanical terms. Intellect may also be less important than the capacity to deal with complexity, to synthesize different ideas, and to articulate the essence of the conversation in a clear and meaningful fashion.

Leadership deals with the emotional and the essential in the outside world. But that work is based on personal energy, drawn from deep within. Once more, leaders connect with others emotionally in a way that energizes them and causes them to act, and they provide the assurance that people need to pursue important values. In my experience – and I'd be interested in yours – the person who leads must sometimes energize others by actively engaging and at other times by being a calming and restorative influence. I'd encourage you to watch for these two equally dynamic expressions of energy in your own leadership and that of others.

Social Energy

Let's look at social energy. For you as a leader, coming up with good ideas will rarely be enough. People can get interested in "explanations," but they are rarely energized without some kind of emotional commitment. You must evoke an emotional response so that people will become active and engaged. Only when people are "moved" emotionally will they begin to "move" psychologically and physically.

At the center is the perspective that leaders bring to their work. They simply understand the social world in a unique way. Where others see a pattern of human desires, leaders see a pattern of human aspirations. Where others see a group of individuals, leaders see a field of relationships. Where others just see people talking, leaders see a field of social energy, waiting to be tapped. Leaders see the aspirations, capabilities, and promise of group members as the raw material to build the emerging narrative of the group. In that respect, and through engaging in extensive conversations, you can come to know the group in an especially intimate way, recognizing patterns of intentions and action that even members of the group don't see. You are a part of the group, but in a sense, you also stand outside the group. From that vantage point, you can see and record things, bringing a special perspective to the life of the group.

As already noted, your role is not just to accept at face value the group's purpose and direction but to reframe the group's story. Your contribution to the dialogue is to inspire reflection and change through insight and creativity. The narrative returned to the group is in part reflection, in part invention.

You must also offer a purpose and direction so compelling that people are energized, moved to act. The expression of purpose and action in that direction are inevitably intertwined so that one cannot exist without the other. They are joined together, and at that moment, people are energized. This is the ancient philosophical notion of "praxis" – the coming together of theory and practice, reflection and action.

For the leader, developing genuine human relationships is the key. But these are different from the transactions or exchanges that are found in most organizations. Traditional approaches to organizations depend on transactions or exchanges, such as "I'll do this for you if you'll do this for me," or the even more basic "I'll provide pay and other incentives if you do the work." These transactions provide the basis for management work: manipulating exchanges of value in order to accomplish given objectives.

But acts of leading can't be based on simple transactions alone. They require deeper human relationships, because such relationships contain the hidden emotional wires and cables that transmit personal energy and transform it into social energy.

As a leader, you must have a capacity for designing and shaping relationships as they move through space and time. To work with these patterns, you must be able to see, not just the "dots," but ways of "connecting the dots." Of course, you will work with individuals and groups, but what is more important are the relationships you will encounter – the exchange of human energy between and among people.

Imagine a beach ball bouncing around a room of people. The beach ball represents the flow of conversations, and its path represents relationships. Knowledge of the capabilities and concerns of the individuals is important. While the leader takes note of individual players, the pattern of relationships, the path, may be ultimately more telling than the individuals who are batting the ball around.

Think of a basketball team going through the course of a game. The players' actions are bound by a specific space and a specific time, the court and the clock. But these are merely backdrops against which the players structure bursts of energy that flow through time and space. One of the important roles of the leader is to organize the flow of energy in a way to best advance the group's purpose.

Consider the United States' 1960s' ambition to put a man on the Moon. You may have read about how President John Kennedy's expression of that goal had the effect of restructuring the way we thought about space and time, both in the sense of how we understood distances and travel times between the Earth and the Moon and how we might organize our political and organizational time and space over the next several years.

Moreover, because people responded to the emotional challenge that the president presented, much greater social and political "energy" was focused on the space program. The primary effect of the president's leadership was to "trigger" certain activities undertaken through newly energized groups and organizations.

An additional skill of the leader is the ability to see the whole "field," something that is a very special capability of the most effective leaders. Think of the way some athletes seem to see the field of play better than others. They have a "sense" of the game that derives, at least in part, from knowing where everything is and where everything is going. Hockey great Wayne Gretzky, for example, is supposed to have said roughly, "Others skate to where the puck is; I skate to where the puck is going to be."

For many leaders, and certainly for almost all managers, there is a tendency to think of time and space in rigid terms, epitomized in the organization's chart, the ultimate spatial representation of how the organization is supposed to operate. Of course, what is completely missing from the chart is any sense of movement, any variation in focus or balance or flow, any dynamism, any energy.

In contrast, the leader's field is open, active, and responsive. It involves a sometimes maddening mix of bodies and personalities, of ideas and images, of projects and proposals, all coming together in the most unpredictable ways. When these forces crystallize in perfect action, in harmony with one another, there is a sense of "flow." Things feel right, and people feel good. When they don't, groups, organizations, and societies falter, and sometimes they even collapse.

Energy then is not just that which moves the body and leads to sweat and sore muscles. Rather, energy is the coming together of time and space, pattern and purpose, so that an inner intention is translated into external action. Expressing the aspirations of the group, building human relationships that carry emotional energy, and facilitating the flow of that energy through time and space – that's what leadership is all about.

Moral Energy

We've talked about personal energy and social energy. What about moral energy?

The best leaders have the capacity to identify our yearnings and our passions (even when we are unaware of them), and then to articulate those as aspirations for the future. The world of those who lead at whatever level is inherently one in which they are living "on the edge," the edge of the present as it falls into the future. And that's, of course, where values and value choices abound.

Many people, perhaps most, would say that leadership is neutral with respect to ethics, in the sense that skills of effective leadership can be used for any purpose – for good or for evil. The classic question of whether Hitler was a leader is often used to make this point, with most people saying that Hitler was indeed a leader, mobilizing a whole nation in pursuit of his grand ambitions. Others would say, however, his pursuits were based on evil intentions, and therefore, he was not a real leader. By taking the position that Hitler was a leader, people are saying that what the leader is trying to achieve is irrelevant to leadership per se.

I disagree. I think that every action a leader takes, whether in discussing the group's purpose or direction or helping to shape the actions of the group, is cut through with moral and ethical consequences. The intent of the leader may, in fact, be the most important factor in judging the ethics of leadership.

Certainly, people in prominent positions often do bad things: they lie, they cheat, they steal, they treat people unjustly. Most of these moral lapses are not based on a conscious choice to "break a rule" or, more generally, to promote evil rather than good. Often the person doing evil doesn't even know at the time that he or she is doing evil. Most leaders don't make ethical mistakes based solely on greed or callousness, though some do.

Rather, most fail to see moral issues that are inherent in a situation but lie just beneath the surface. They uncritically accept an organization's culture and fail to recognize the ethical traps it holds for them. They neglect low-probability events, they miscalculate risks, they fail to consider all the parties that might be involved, and they downplay long-term consequences. They allow themselves to be blinded by opportunity, and don't see the negatives. They arrive at a point where they say, "We've gotten ourselves into a situation where we can't get out. We have to do whatever we can to save the organization – and save ourselves." They may be tempted to lie to followers or at least spin the truth to conceal what they are doing.

But many people in many settings lie, cheat, and steal. These transgressions are not exclusive to leaders. But there are at least a couple of ways in which leadership itself might be deemed unethical: first, when leadership is exercised to benefit the leader rather than the community; and second, when leadership is exercised in a way that is biased, deceptive, manipulative, or secretive. Obviously, the two are closely tied.

Leadership cannot occur without intention. Meaningful human action is always intentional, and we can make moral judgments about those intentions. Some people lead in order to advance their own personal agenda, seeking notoriety or, even more likely, financial gain. Others lead to promote the narrow political bias of one social group at the expense of others. But leadership based on self-interest or on a narrowly defined political interest is morally questionable.

Leading in order to gain power or money invites the kind of personal indiscretions mentioned earlier. Leading according to self-interest can also push the leader into using power and manipulation, both of which raise the moral question of whether one human being should have the right to compel others to abandon what might be in their own best interest so as to follow the leader.

There's one special danger that is connected to self-interested leadership, and that is charisma, the personal magnetism that some leaders have that leads to an almost spiritual devotion on the part of followers. Again, some argue that charisma itself is neutral and can be used for good or evil. However, I would say that charismatic leadership in whatever its form constitutes a moral "slippery slope."

On the one hand, a charismatic leader may be tempted to use his or her allure for personal gain or to make decisions based on conceit rather than reason. On the other, the followers may be put in the position of unwittingly and uncritically accepting the values of the leader; they may be too easily manipulated. Again, Hitler is often used as the classic example of charismatic manipulation. But, in any case, leadership based on self-interest fails; leading on behalf of the broad interests of the larger community is far more compelling.

Taking this position, James MacGregor Burns, in his classic book *Leadership*, argued that leadership involves a relationship between leaders and followers who engage with one another in a process of determining what is to be sought. For moral leadership to occur, the values of both the leader and the followers must be represented. Burns writes, "Leaders and followers are engaged in a common enterprise; they are dependent on each other, their fortunes rise and fall together."

In this relationship, the views of your followers should be freely expressed and fully entertained. You should engage in a dialogue, not a monologue, and that dialogue should be free of fear, coercion, and even excessive influence. It should be structured so that fundamentally new ideas and possibilities will emerge.

As a leader, one of your primary tasks is to create an open and visible process through which members of the group can express their needs and interests; in other words, you need to maintain the integrity of the group process. Moreover, you need to be sensitive to the values at play in any leadership situation. Developing the capacity to see the key operative values in a group and to articulate the ethical dilemmas involved is what we call "moral imagination."

Moral imagination does not mean the application of preexisting rules or ethical standards. Rather, it suggests that the leader (along with others) brings focus to ethical issues, which may then be resolved based on a process of discourse and negotiation within the community. In this sense, codes of morality are not "handed down from on high" – that is, from religious, political, or managerial elites. Instead, they are living and evolving records, always subject to discussion and reevaluation by the community at large. At its best, such a process is expressive, collaborative, and transparent.

Developing this capacity requires that you, as a leader, assume a certain responsibility, the responsibility to make sure that resolving moral issues is undertaken with care, openness, and sensitivity.

There are sufficient issues out there to occupy your attention, and many will be brought to you in very direct fashion. For example, issues of discrimination may come to you based on gender, race, and ethnicity, and you must be prepared to address such issues directly. In fact, using your sense of moral imagination, you should confront these issues, squarely and purposefully, even before someone brings them to your attention. Being out in front on moral issues not only works to your advantage, but it's the right thing to do.

I have discussed personal energy, social energy, and moral energy. To put the pieces back together again: as a leader, you must express personal energy in a way that excites the energy of others in pursuit of moral purposes.

Yours,

Bob

12
LETTER FROM KAYLA
December 14

Dr. Bob

Thanks for your comments on the significance of energy in leadership. I would not have thought of trying to analyze what goes on in our organization in terms of energy, but now that you have brought it up, I can't seem to avoid doing so. There are examples everywhere. It's like having a new set of glasses that allow me to see things that I didn't see before. I think I remember your saying in class that managers focus on the actions of individuals and groups, while leaders focus on the relationship among individuals and groups. Another way of saying that would be to say that leaders focus on the energy exchanged among people.

I've had fun recently trying to study the interplay of energy in groups at work. It's opened up a whole new world to me.

It's amazing how focusing on energy rather than the actions of individual people gives you a whole new way of seeing what's happening. I'll try to write more about that soon, but wanted to pick up on a couple of ideas that have been floating around in my head.

I happened to see our CEO, Robert, last week. (He asked about our letters and sent greetings to you.) You may know that I first met Robert at a job fair at the university and he eventually recruited me to work for his company. I've felt he's been watching over me ever since, and I find that comforting. We chatted about my future with the company and he was very encouraging. Robert even mentioned positions I might hold at some point, and that gave me a better sense of how I might progress in the company.

He also urged me to take advantage of leadership development opportunities – and incidentally thought you might have some ideas about which programs would be best for me. He also suggested that I hire an executive coach and gave me the name of Brenda Simmons as a possibility. He even offered to pay for some of this!

Robert is very big on having people think carefully about leadership before moving into those leadership "positions" and, while he still uses that term, I think he understands your point about leading as something that is needed throughout an organization. He's very supportive of leadership development, as I think any good leader, or should I say, any top executive should be. Though I don't see him as often as I would like, I think of Robert as both a mentor and a champion for me. And an excellent leader.

For some reason, that makes me think once again about the criticisms of millennials, including that they (we?) shift from job to job too rapidly. I don't think that's really what's happening. I don't plan to move from this organization as long as it is providing good developmental opportunities for me. Investing time and money in potential leaders, as Robert is doing, is the right approach to keeping millennials in the organization, just as it is the right approach to keeping anyone else.

This is something that I would like to communicate to more senior managers. "Young folks" aren't all that different. I suppose I might be ready to move more than some of my senior colleagues. But just like them, I want to go where the opportunities are and where I have good support for the work I do.

And one more piece of advice for our senior colleagues. As a friend of mine put it, "We're not the enemy," though treating us that way may make us so. We have a lot to contribute. We, both millennials and more senior people, need to spend some time figuring out how we are different and how we can each use our strengths to see and address problems others may miss. And seeing those differences and the different strengths that we bring to the job might enable us all to perform more effectively.

Just a few comments that I hope will be helpful.

Kayla

13
LETTER FROM MIKE
December 15

Bob

    I was in Los Angeles on business last week and arranged to have lunch with Kayla while I was there. She told me about the note that she sent to you, but which I had not yet seen. She was especially eager to talk about the three modes of energy that you discussed in your last letter.

    At her urging, we played a game during lunch – to track patterns of energy in the restaurant. The first thing we noticed was that early on the energy level in the room was fairly low, but as more people crowded in, you could sense the change. There was more buzz, more tension, and more excitement. Any other time I would have failed to notice this as a shift in energy, probably just thinking that the noise level had increased. But by paying attention, I became aware of different levels of energy in different parts of the room, and the different expressions of energy in various places. I'm not sure how to describe the differences – active versus passive, engaged or disengaged, hot versus cold, stable or unstable, etc.

    The flow of energy was even more apparent as we focused on specific people in the room. At one point, the manager/hostess, was trying to accommodate a large group by moving several tables around. But one of the two waiters who were helping, backed into a customer seated nearby, almost causing him to spill his soup. The two waiters thought this was hilarious. The manager remained calm and said nothing, other than apologizing to the customer. But you could see the daggers of energy she was directing at the waiters. They noticed and acted as if their electricity had just been turned off. In a way it had.

    At that moment, a somewhat heated discussion broke out at the counter between the wait staff and the kitchen staff, something about an over-cooked entrée. The manager was all the way across the room and facing away, but she clearly sensed the disruption in the flow of energy in the room and immediately moved to the counter to calm people down. Somehow her presence seemed to moderate the situation. She was calm but firm, and a new, even energy returned.

As the manager went back toward the front door, she stopped briefly at one table to give a special welcome to some important guests (or guests she wanted to make feel important). You could visibly see the energy level at that table rise. And when the manager finally got to her stand, you could see her expressing appreciation to her young assistant for carrying on so well in her brief absence and, as you might expect, he registered his pleasure with a clear boost in energy.

As Kayla and I discussed what we had been watching, we were not only further convinced of the importance of tracking the energy in a group or organization, but also how much our own energy was dependent on our interactions with others and vice versa. We find some people naturally energizing and others less so. And that's our definition of leadership, isn't it!

Kayla also remembered that you had talked about rhythm as a way of making sense of group interactions and we spent some time thinking about the connection between rhythm and energy, both of which normally exhibit a steady beat or wave, but which can be stimulated to significant levels of excitement. And, speaking of waves, we thought about the ocean, sometimes gently lapping against the shore and other times crashing recklessly inland.

I guess energy can be used for good purposes or bad, depending on the intent of the individual. But, in any case, there's much to be learned from watching the energy flow back and forth among the members of a group or organization. I think we will both remember this insight for a long time. Thanks.

Mike

P.S. Our family will be traveling to visit relatives during the holidays. May I suggest that we take a break from our writing until about the middle of January?

14

LETTER FROM BOB

January 15

Dear Kayla and Mike,

I hope that you had wonderful holidays and that, like me, you're eager to get back to our letters.

I've been thinking that, at this point, grouping some letters and having you respond to a larger set makes some sense. It allows me to examine several aspects of an issue at once and gives you a little break in terms of reading and writing. Let me outline the topics that I want to discuss in the next four letters.

In this letter and the next, I'll discuss genuinely human relationships, in the one following, I'll discuss using purpose and direction rather than vision, and in the fourth of this set, I will consider the skills that are needed for a new way of leading. As I said, I think it would make sense for you to wait for all four of these letters before responding, though feel free to write at any time.

Also, from this point forward, I would like to make a small shift in focus. We have characterized leadership (the act of leading) as something that can occur in many different settings. But I think the process of leading is significantly altered by time, the culture, or the setting you are in. This means that we might focus on "leadership on the playground," "leadership in politics," or "leadership in organization" (or many others). I don't want us to forget that point. It's extremely important. But I would like for us to focus most of our attention on leadership in organizations, meaning by that, leadership in all kinds of public, private, and nonprofit organizations.

In doing so, we shouldn't make the mistake of assuming that the leader is by definition the top executive. Rather we will see organizations as having multiple leaders throughout the organization. Leadership can and should be widely distributed both vertically and horizontally. So, when I talk about leaders' relationship-building, or visioning, or skill-building, I intend for what I say to apply to leadership at all levels. Let's start somewhere near the middle of an organization.

Kim's Story

I have already suggested that tomorrow's leaders will need to be more and more attentive to relationships. I'd like to illustrate that point by sharing the story of an emerging leader who learned that lesson the hard way.

A neighbor of mine, whom we'll call Kim – since that's her name – attended a small liberal arts college in Nebraska, then landed a much-sought-after position in a large financial firm. After a couple of years, Kim enrolled in an executive MBA program at Penn State. There, Kim spent most of her time engaged in highly quantitative courses in accounting, microeconomics, financial management, operations management, and business strategy.

Along the way, she had one course in management and organizational behavior, which she found a little "fluffy." But most of her coursework was quite relevant to the financial analysis work she was doing. Her investment in the program (which was not cheap) really seemed to be paying off. She learned a lot of helpful tools and techniques, and she earned a prestigious degree that would surely help her back home. Everything seemed to be going well.

Soon, she found herself on the fast track, one of only a few of her counterparts selected for job rotations, international postings, and advanced analytic training. In these roles, she became more polished in her relations with her coworkers and began to "dress for success," trying to match the professional image of her senior colleagues, even though most were men. She thought she looked splendid in her new blue suit from Nordstrom's. She even hired an executive coach to help her in navigating the organizational maze.

In quiet moments at home, she wondered what it would be like to lead the company or at least one of its major divisions. In high school and college, she had been considered a leader, or at least someone who could get things done. She was often praised for her ability to organize a task and to make rational and objective decisions, even under pressure. She didn't think of herself as especially ambitious or power hungry, but the image of her occupying a corner office kept creeping into her mind.

However, there were more immediate things to worry about.

Throughout her MBA program, she felt she had the strong support of her manager, Bill. When Kim was first hired, she thought of Bill as the ideal manager or leader – careful, rational, and kind at the same time. Now, Bill seemed to be growing increasingly distant, spending less time in casual conversations with those in the office and displaying a more secretive and controlling style of management. Kim and several of her coworkers had begun to complain about being left out of the communications "loop" and not feeling as if they understood where Bill was "coming from." Bill was a great sports fan, and several characterized him as being "in a slump."

One day, Bill called Kim into his office, and while he finished a phone call, she looked around the room at the sports trophies, smelled a hint of cigar tobacco, and thought about the slump metaphor. But she still wasn't prepared for what happened. Turning away from the phone, and not even saying hello, Bill gave Kim what she considered a completely "out of the blue" dressing down, suggesting she was "in over her head," and chastizing her as excessively ambitious, even suggesting her focus on personal advancement was getting in the way of her assigned work duties. He particularly focused on one project that Kim had undertaken but had failed to complete in time because, he suggested, she was away from the office pursuing her own ambitions.

Kim was stunned and left Bill's office shaking visibly. She thought she had been doing exactly what was expected of her. For example, the manager above Bill, a senior VP named Tony, had been encouraging her to engage in the various "advancement" programs that the company offered and, indeed, had hinted at a significant promotion that might be coming up. And the project that Bill talked about – that was a minor report that anyone could have done overnight. Indeed, she had done it overnight, only a day or two after it was originally due.

And what about Bill? For months, it had appeared that he was playing political games in the office, bending the truth in his reports to his manager and telling one thing to one person and something else to another. Perhaps he was angling for some kind of promotion himself, but he seemed like a different person – tenser, more scheming, and now and then downright mean. Maybe there was something happening in Bill's life that Kim didn't know about or understand, but he was making her increasingly uncomfortable, even miserable.

Kim talked with her mother and a few friends, all of whom took her side and were critical of Bill and his actions. Some even suggested that this was the time for Kim to start looking for another job where she would be happier and more productive. After all, she was now well trained and had a strong record with the company, though she was worried about what Bill might say if someone from a headhunting firm or another company contacted him about her work. On the other hand, she felt she had an ally in Tony, and she began to find more opportunities to spend time on work she knew he was interested in.

One day following a meeting, Kim and Tony were walking together back toward their offices, and he asked about how Bill was doing. Kim hesitated, not wanting to undercut Bill (or at least not wanting to be perceived as undercutting Bill). But Tony had always been straightforward with her, and she decided to tell him what she really thought. It wasn't pretty. Tony listened carefully, then said, "Kim, I wasn't asking about Bill's work. I was asking about his health. You know he's been diagnosed with cancer, don't you?" Kim shook her head, then apologized for having to leave so quickly and darted out the next door.

Her first thoughts were about Bill, in part feeling bad about his illness, but also wondering what would happen if he was no longer able to work. An opportunity? But she soon also realized she had just made a major mistake with Tony. Her one champion would at least have doubts about her diplomacy, and at worst would see her as trying to sabotage Bill for her own political ends. This was a disaster.

Good Relationships Gone Bad

Kim's story is not uncommon. It's the story of good relationships gone bad. If you listen to people tell their workplace stories, just as I've told Kim's, you will soon conclude that every member of every organization has relationship issues. And that conclusion would be correct. The relationships among people are absolutely essential to effective and responsible performance, but as relationships break apart, they cause great damage. They cause pain to individuals, and they limit organizational effectiveness.

While we all have relationship problems, we rarely call them that. Instead, we sanitize them by calling them "communications problems." And they are everywhere. In fact, I've never known an organization where people didn't complain about communications problems. And I bet you haven't either. But these communications problems are often really problems of power, over-reaching, information-hoarding, or some combination of all of these. It's not that people don't communicate effectively (though they often don't); the deeper, more systemic problem is that organizations have built-in mechanisms that inhibit effective human communications.

We are pretty good at diagnosing and even repairing ordinary communications problems, such as not speaking clearly, not listening carefully, not clarifying ambiguous messages, or not confirming points of view. We resolve these concerns through techniques such as active listening and supportive communications. But there are deeper problems in communications that interfere with relationship-building, some embedded in the very structure of human organizations.

Traditional organizations are ritualized structures of power and authority, and in these organizations, power trumps communications. One thing that happens is that people shape their conversations based on whether the other person is one they perceive as having power or not having power. Consider how your "story" changes when you are talking with someone with more power than you as opposed to someone with the same power. You avoid being the one who brings the bad news; you align your proposals with what you think the one in power wants to hear; you "pad" your own accomplishments, thinking that may help with promotions or raises.

And it works the other way around. You are likely to talk differently with someone whom you consider a subordinate. At the same time, they are shaping their comments based on your power position.

Here's another illustration: imagine a top-management-team planning session in which all are present and involved, including the chief executive. Whose ideas do you think will be given precedence?

Alternatively, imagine the same session with ideas and information being anonymously typed into a messaging system and shared with all. No one knows which message comes from which person. In this case, you would expect that the best ideas would "win," whether they are from the most powerful or not (or maybe the winner is the fastest typist!).

Other issues are caused by the fact that different people have access to different information: almost everyone knows something others don't – and wants to know things they think others know. And, admittedly, some of these problems are caused by the fact that we're simply human. We have our own perceptions of things going on around us and our own emotional triggers. We respond differently to the same information. And we change our minds – often.

All of this becomes more complicated by the fact that greater pay, higher status, and other accoutrements are associated with movement up the ladder. But remember that the reason for the ladder itself is that different rungs are steps to greater power. (The tangible benefits associated with the top positions did not create power – it was power that created them.)

Ambition is often the driving force in moving up, but ambition comes in many colors. There certainly are many people whose ambitions are grounded in their desire to benefit the community, to make a positive difference in the world. There are others who are attracted to positions of power by the promise of better compensation or greater status. And I do think some people, maybe many people, seek power for its own sake. But whatever the motive that underlies their ambition, when they arrive at a higher position, they have more power. And if organizations continue to be structured as they currently are, they will use that power.

Sometimes they will engage in conscious exercises of power, occasionally even to the point of abuse. At other times, given the fact that power in organizations is so deeply embedded in our culture and consciousness, power holders will use their power without even being aware that they are doing so. And others will submit to power without even being aware that they are doing so. Power has become so taken for granted, so matter of fact that we often don't even recognize it.

In my view, we won't get very far in solving our relationship problems until we address several critical underlying communications issues. And we won't solve our communications problems until we change the way we think about power in organizations.

We have spoken of the importance of engaging with the group as part of the process of leading. For that process to be most successful, communications must be as clear as possible. However, to the extent that the engagement is colored by power, the clear communications essential to effective leadership will be difficult to attain. Our current pattern of organization creates a tension between power and communications, one in which power typically prevails. That is, power limits effective communications, rather than the other way around.

The wise leader will do everything possible to clarify communications, and, in part, that means doing everything possible to minimize the influence of power. As communications become less distorted, people can work together more effectively, and cooperation and collaboration can be increased. As power recedes, genuinely human relationships can be built.

It occurs to me that Mari's leadership on the playground was carried out without power or position, while Cooper, despite his best efforts, could never appear a peer. (Note the clever, or, truthfully, accidental play on words!)

Maybe the best leadership, the leadership of a child, is something that in today's world we have left behind. But maybe tomorrow's leadership and tomorrow's organizations will allow us to return to our more natural and playful patterns of human relationships.

In any case, this is the view from 30,000 feet. What about the world at ground level – that is, at Kim's level? Here, too, the same expectations played out.

Learning about Relationships

First, Kim obviously expected her work life to be rational and objective; she expected everyone else to be the same as her. (Again, to make the assumption that everyone is like you is always a mistake.) She came up short in terms of self-reflection and self-awareness, which she occasionally confused with self-absorption.

Second, without even knowing it, she let her ambition, and maybe even a little thirst for power, get in the way of building effective human relationships, depending instead on transactional relationships.

Third, she didn't really "connect" with those around her, many of whom were giving her clues as to what was going on in the workplace. But their clues were often veiled and protective of Kim – to the point that she didn't get the message. Consequently, she was locked into her own perception of the world.

Incidentally, Bill is not without fault in this story either. While his illness was tragic, it doesn't excuse his toxic behavior with respect to his subordinates. Though the story doesn't address this question, I would bet that he was not as brusque in his relations with Tony or others higher up in the organization. But we do know that he cut himself off from others at a time he most needed genuine human relationships.

Almost every interaction in this story was based on a transactional view of organization – the communication involved a "this-for-that" transaction. In exchange for Tony's support, Kim was willing to go beyond her normal work and take on extra projects. Similarly, as Bill grew less supportive and more distant, Kim withdrew her contributions and started making obvious mistakes.

Meanwhile, Kim's ambitions were largely a secret, and neither Bill nor Tony knew much about where Kim was heading. Bill suspected her of plotting her own way forward, but he was largely blind to what she was doing in this regard. And, of course, Kim wasn't clear in her own mind about her future.

While all three people in the story talked with one another, their conversations were largely superficial – that is, they talked on the surface, while concealing their real motives and intentions. Each person had his or her own agenda and sought individually beneficial exchanges. They accepted power as the currency of the realm: their interactions, their transactions, were always subtly, sometimes even invisibly colored by power.

What is important to realize is that this kind of behavior is not accidental, but rather "built-in" to the traditional model of organization. People are expected to operate within the hierarchical lines of communication. They are expected to play by the rules (policies). For the most part, in traditional organizations, the feelings and emotions are given a back seat.

Everyone in this case was doing exactly what you would expect, given the transactional nature of organizations. They were acting out their games of power and ambition through a series of superficial transactions in which there was almost always a winner and a loser. In this part of the story, Kim and her colleagues all suffered personally as well as organizationally. Their ambitions, their pursuit of positions of power – it's all pretty much the same – left them personally unfulfilled, only satisfied when the pendulum of power swung their way.

Yours,

Bob

15

LETTER FROM BOB

January 20

Dear Kayla and Mike,

What happened to Kim? I'll tell you as much as I know. Remember that Kim had just learned of Bill's health issues and was concerned that she had lost her connection with Tony, her mentor and champion.

More on Kim

As she walked back toward her office, Kim felt an overwhelming sense of remorse. She had failed to see what was right in front of her, even when she had once voiced the possibility that something was troubling Bill and might explain his "slump." Her remorse was amplified by her remembering the stories she had told her mother, stories that were naturally slanted to make her appear the victim.

But what should she do? She could certainly bury herself in her work until the clouds she had created passed on, and then she could get back in the game. She could apologize to Tony for her misunderstanding of his question and hope to win him back over to her side. She could talk with her mother or her coach and devise a plan for moving forward, maybe finding a new job.

Even as she silently considered these options, she had a nagging feeling that it was just this kind of thinking that had gotten her to this point in the first place. Had she been so driven by her emerging ambition that it had eventually led to her downfall?

She had been so wrapped up in her thoughts that she hadn't even noticed that it had started raining. For some reason, as she pulled her hood over her head, she remembered her third-grade teacher, Ms. Barnard (alias "The Barn Yard") – an expansive and particularly fidgety woman, but one who could turn a chance phrase into an important life lesson. It was one of these moments that Kim now recalled. The Barn Yard had concluded a short parable with the lesson, "Do what's right, even if it hurts really bad."

Kim shook off the raindrops and turned toward Bill's office. It was only a short walk.

Bill wasn't in but was expected back momentarily, so Kim was asked to wait at the small round conference table. She looked once more at the sports trophies, thought of her last visit to this office, and almost bolted. But she remained seated.

Fewer than ten minutes later, Bill walked in and, without saying hello, sat across the table. His look was curious, but his voice pleasant enough as he wiped the rain off his glasses and asked why she was there.

Kim hesitated, fumbling with a button on her sleeve, then blurted out, "I've come to apologize."

"For what?" Bill's intense gaze softened with curiosity.

Kim hesitated once more, then softly said, "I'm not really sure." Another long pause, then, "For being a jerk. For thinking too much about myself. For not taking the time to see what was going on with others. With you."

Bill relaxed noticeably, leaned back in his chair, and quietly said, "Thank you. We may both be guilty of that. How about some lunch and a conversation?"

A Hint of Sunshine

As they left the building, both Kim and Bill noticed that the rain had nearly stopped and that a hint of sunshine was peeking through the clouds. Both acknowledged the improved weather with a smile and a nod, but other than that, they walked in silence to a nearby café.

Sitting in a corner booth, they ordered drinks and clung quietly to their menus until the waiter took their order. After another long silence, Kim opened the conversation by asking about Bill's health and apologizing for not recognizing what was going on sooner.

Bill recounted in considerable detail what he had been through over the last six months, including both the physical and financial demands his illness had placed on him and on his family. He seemed relieved to finally be able to tell the story.

Meanwhile, Kim listened carefully and occasionally nodded her understanding and sympathy. Yet through it all, she had to fight the feeling of being removed from the actual situation, almost observing it clinically from the outside.

Bill coasted to a stopping place and then courteously asked about what had been going on in Kim's life.

Kim at first demurred, saying, "Not much." But with a little further prompting from Bill, she described her increasing preoccupation with her own career advancement.

"It's that power thing, isn't it?" Bill remarked. "That took hold of me a few years ago and just wouldn't let go. But cancer has a way of refocusing your attention. Unfortunately, it also has a way of pointing out your limitations. It can make you downright mean, can't it?"

"Well, we were wondering if you were in a slump," Kim ventured, hoping to add a little lightness to the conversation.

"It was worse than that, wasn't it?" Bill replied.

Kim dodged the question by moving back to her own situation, acknowledging how little attention she had paid to others over the past several months and, consequentially, how self-centered she had been.

The conversation continued with the confessional tone until, at some point, one of the two – Kim couldn't remember who it was – remarked on how comical they were in their self-pity. "Any priest who heard this avalanche of confessions would simply say, 'Get over it!'"

They both laughed nervously, and as they finished their meal and started back to the office, they promised more frequent lunches and helpful conversations.

Neither Kim nor Bill felt that anything had been resolved during their lunch, but both considered it the beginning of a new way of working with one another. They returned to their respective offices, attended meetings, answered e-mails, and signed off on various requests. But their hearts weren't in it that day.

We can only speculate as to what happened next. Certainly, Kim made a good start in righting her relationship with Bill, but doing so was very difficult. It involved Kim's making herself extraordinarily vulnerable, perhaps even so vulnerable that her story stretches credibility. But Bill was open to her gesture and greeted it empathetically, recognizing in her vulnerability his own and reaching out to her. For a moment, both Kim's and Bill's subtle preoccupations receded, and the possibility of real human connection appeared.

On the other hand, the story illustrates exactly the way that power distorts communications. Certainly, Kim expressed her ideas differently to Bill and to Tony than she did to her mother and her friends. Bill, on the other hand, very likely communicated differently with Tony and others with more power than he did with Kim and others at her level.

I don't think it really matters whether we call Kim's motive "ambition" or a "drive for power" because they amount to the same thing and, if they are successful, lead to the same result. What Bill called "the power thing" could have easily been called "the ambition thing." In most traditional organizations, ambition means seeking higher offices, which is the same as seeking more power.

Whether the new connection blossomed into a healthy human relationship – and, no, I don't mean an affair – is something we'll probably never know because Kim moved out of our neighborhood soon after these events occurred, and I can't find her phone, address, or e-mail.

Healthy Relationships

Certainly any organization founded on the principles of hierarchical power and, growing from that, justifying severe differences in status and pay, is not one in which you would expect healthy human relationships to flourish. As long as organizations are built on transactions rather than human relationships, they will remain tied to and limited by the same commitment to power and rationality that Kim exhibited in her early days at the company.

On the other hand, to the extent that healthy human relationships replace transactions as the basis for organizational life, the possibility of new connections will be greatly improved. Moreover, to the extent that communications free of power replace those shaped by power, we would expect more open communications, collaboration, and even productive conflict.

In such a circumstance, the necessity to manage human behavior will decrease, and the opportunity for real leadership will increase. Kayla and Mike, it is important that you and others in your situation understand this completely: organizations of the future will be led, not managed. Or to say that more accurately, people of the future will be led, not managed.

I realize that this image of the future may appear to be sheer fantasy to some. But just as such technologies as smartphones were science fiction only a few decades ago, why shouldn't we be able to change the limiting patterns of human behavior that we find in today's groups and organizations? Why shouldn't we be able to open up new opportunities for us to develop our fullest human potential?

Such changes may not keep pace with the rapidity of technological change. Indeed, as I suggested earlier, dramatic changes in the way that we lead and organize are likely to take hundreds of years. But I think the direction of those changes is now set for you and other emerging leaders and not likely to be redirected: transactions will be replaced by relationships, domination will be replaced by autonomy, and power will be replaced by communications. It may be a long time coming, but it's on the way.

Yours,

Bob

16
LETTER FROM MIKE
January 22

Dear Bob

I don't want to interrupt the flow of your writing but I have some news about the job in Los Angeles. The company made an attractive offer, and, in fact, improved that offer as we went along, but ultimately I turned it down. In economic terms the new position would have been quite an advancement – the salary and benefits were almost in the "Wow" category.

But as Annie and I talked about moving and as we heard from friends and colleagues here and elsewhere, we just felt it wasn't the right time to move. It certainly was an attractive offer, and the opportunities to lead in important work were substantial, but in the end, it just wasn't me, it just wasn't us!

So, I'm settling back into my current position, though occasionally wondering if we made the right decision. Meanwhile, I'm going to try to get back into the rhythm of my job and the rhythm of our correspondence, and see if I can be helpful as we explore a new way of thinking about leadership.

Mike

17

LETTER FROM BOB

January 25

Dear Kayla and Mike,

I've been traveling some recently, both to visit family in Delaware and to discuss some of these ideas with friends and colleagues in Pennsylvania. But I did receive your letters and I want to respond here to a couple of the points that you made.

First, however, Mike, I'm sorry things didn't work out for you in LA, but it sounds like you made a good decision – by which I mean a good choice made for the right reasons. So, it's back to work without the distraction of job hunting. You commented on the reverse "buyer's remorse" that you are feeling now. It's certainly difficult for men and women in our society to reject offers of good jobs that seem to provide advancement, prestige, and, more money.

As I've mentioned before, I think your generation is much better about prioritizing meaningful work and family connections than mine. But the transition hasn't fully come about, and consequently, saying "no" to an offer like the one you had is difficult. However, I thought you summed up the choice in an excellent fashion when you said, "It just wasn't me. It just wasn't us."

Mike, several letters back you reminded us that I had avoided using the word "vision" in describing the process of energizing a group or organization, even though, as you remarked, vision is probably the one word most often used to describe what leaders do. You even noted (correctly) that I had only used the word "vision" in arguing against the use of vision as a defining feature of leadership. Let me try to explain why.

Years ago, when you were very young, probably even before you were born, President George H. W. Bush was criticized for not having what one columnist called "a clarity of ideas and principles." The president then offhandedly remarked on "the vision thing," a phrase that caught on and indeed has become an essential part of the lexicon of leadership. When people are asked what constitutes leadership, they will almost always say something, as you did, about vision – that the leader is the one with the vision and the one with the power to move the organization toward that vision. But let's take a more critical look at "the vision thing."

For most organizations today, the process of setting a vision is usually done through some sort of strategic planning process, sometimes a formal process involving many stakeholders, though more often an informal process in which the organization's founders or those at the top simply create and send out their vision for the organization. In either case, the vision is a long-term statement of the desired future and is typically elaborated by a mission statement, which explains the rationale of the organization and the means of achieving the vision. Based on the mission statement, more specific objectives are then developed.

At a practical level, of course, many groups and organizations create (or unveil) a new statement of vision, experience about three weeks of buzz, then ignore the vision, and go on their way. There are several reasons for this.

First, some plans are simply not implementable; they bear little relevance to the actual work "on the ground." This is most likely to happen when the plans are formulated at the top of the organization and simply handed down through the ranks. The rationale for doing so is that the chief executive can see "the big picture" of where the organization has been and where it is going, while those near the bottom have a limited view.

But those on the front line will usually recognize, more quickly than those at the top, the differences between the plan and the realities it will face. There are dramatic differences between the "view from the top" and the "view from the bottom." While those at the top claim to see the big picture, theirs is a picture that lacks detail and often assumes irrelevant detail. Meanwhile, those at the bottom see a more accurate picture, a more nuanced and concrete picture. They know when the plan faces "contrary realities."

Second, many plans are almost immediately outdated, either because the real world, the world of action, ebbs and flows in unpredictable and uncontrollable ways, or simply because things change. Boxing fans know the old quotation, usually attributed to Mike Tyson, that "Everyone has a plan – until they get punched in the mouth." To put that in a business context, Amazon CEO Jeff Bezos remarked, "Any plan won't survive its first encounter with reality. The reality will always be different. It will never be the plan." And when this happens, the plan becomes irrelevant and simply takes up shelf space (or computer "trash" space) and the company has to move on.

In a world in which change is the only constant, planners can rarely anticipate all the shifting circumstances the organization will face. Business competitors come up with new ideas and bring them to market right away, leaving your company holding the (empty) bag. Elections swing in different directions from those anticipated and government agencies must respond in the moment. New information comes to light from the other side of the world that precludes the organization from moving on its planned course. The more things stay the same, the more they change. And often the planners simply can't keep up.

Third, and sometimes even worse, is the opposite effect – that groups and organizations become so tied to their initial vision that it acts as a straitjacket, preventing members of the group from recognizing emerging trends and responding to those new circumstances. Many startups fail precisely because their founders are so wedded to their original idea, so psychologically committed, that they fail to see that what they hope to accomplish is unachievable or has already been done by someone else, preempting the market. Often, just a slight deviation from the vision would have saved the company.

Certainly, groups and organizations need a direction or a path to start out on, but they also need adaptability – the flexibility to recognize when they need to move in a new direction or take a new path. In opposition to tunnel vision, they need peripheral vision – the ability to see the big picture, including emerging threats and opportunities. They need agility – the capacity to learn and to change directions in both a nimble and sophisticated way. Indeed, I would say that agility and adaptability will trump vision and plan every time.

Fourth, in my view, vision is simply not essential to leadership. Earlier we questioned the idea of having a vision as a definition of leadership and suggested that vision might not even be necessary for leadership to occur. What is essential is engaging the members of the group or organization to draw out the substance and insight that allows you to articulate a purpose and direction. The opposite strategy – having a vision or mission imposed by the person or group in charge – may generate early excitement, though people may also react negatively to the top-down nature of its presentation. In either case, a vision handed down from above will eventually suck energy away from the group or organization, in part because others will recognize that the vision has little relevance to their work "on the ground."

Finally, and often as a result of its irrelevance, a vision can quickly turn into fantasy. Just as many other "positives" carry with them the seeds of their "negatives," so it is with vision. Merriam-Webster cites the following synonyms for vision: chimera, conceit, daydream, delusion, fancy, figment, hallucination, illusion, phantasm, pipe dream, unreality, fantasy. How many visions have you seen that turn out to be delusion or fantasy?

Alternatives to Vision

What are the alternatives to "the vision thing" as it is currently constructed? I would suggest three correctives.

First, the idea of a vision as an "end state" should be replaced by the ideas of "purpose" and "direction," perhaps with a set of accompanying values or principles guiding subsequent actions. Most vision statements today tell employees little about what they should do today or tomorrow. It's only when the vision is rationalized that specific steps emerge, but that process drains the vision of its energy and turns it into uninspiring technique.

Statements of purpose and direction speak more directly to the present as well as the future. Setting objectives requires that we conceive of an end state, then work backwards to where we begin. Statement of purpose and direction start at the beginning. They help us understand how to get started. They ask that we think strategically but act immediately.

In my view, your responsibility as a leader is not to set a vision. Instead, you should set a tone for clear conversation and dialogue in the organization, providing example, clarity, and insight. You should work with others to bring forth the best ideas, those that will guide the organization going forward.

One of Fast Company's "Generation Flux" exemplars, Angela Blanchard, CEO of the Houston Neighborhood Centers, told me that, in her experience, purpose and direction are more compelling than vision. "Values and purpose sustain us as we navigate chaotic climates. What keeps me clear is a set of beliefs about people and the world we live in. The 'how' changes constantly as learning occurs, as new information comes to us, as experimentation pays off. What doesn't change is the 'why' of our work."

Second, a sense of purpose and direction can retain the inspirational or emotive energy that leadership requires, but it can also bring clarity concerning key issues facing the organization. An alternative to tying vision to a rational planning process is what my friend Ralph Kerle calls "envisioning." He writes: "Skillful envisioning uses imagination instead of problem-solving to direct the creative flow in an organization, articulating purpose in a manner that has the power to bring employees, stakeholders, and customers together to create meaningful futures."

In contrast to rational planning, Kerle is describing an aesthetic process for setting the group's purpose and direction, something far more likely to retain the energizing power of leadership than rational planning.

Another aspect of this process, in fact, one of the very most important is the capacity of the leader to take complex material and boil it down to its essence – to be able to state what is really important in a short but meaningful (even memorable) fashion. One corporate CEO told me, "Managers make things complex; leaders make things simple." To state the organization's purpose and direction in terms that are clear and meaningful, using words that "connect," is an essential aspect of leadership because it brings together aspiration and inspiration.

A third element that comes into play in developing purpose and direction is flexibility, and with it, reflexivity. Once more from Angela Blanchard: "You must move through this chaotic, fast-changing world with an eye for an opportunity – focusing on what works and what is strong, using what's available to build something better, faster, more effective. It is not about choosing to be either flexible or consistent; it's about being flexible and consistent at the same time."

As a leader, you must maintain an openness to change and the flexibility to adapt to new circumstances. At the same time, you must be consistent in your purpose, your values, and your principles.

Dinah Boyd, chief researcher at Microsoft, agrees: "I don't think it makes sense to use a North Star metaphor to think about vision. Yes, a long-term vision has inspirational value, but it should not be static. What is static in my mind are core values. I view my values as my North Star and am acutely aware of how my practices and vision change over time, even when my core values do not."

The key to aligning your actions with your values is reflexivity, the capacity for self-reflection and self-critique. Reflexivity, at both the personal and organizational levels, is what makes real, meaningful, and enduring change possible within the confines of your values and commitments.

Self-reflection and self-critique are essential to learning, and learning is essential to flexibility. You must be able to assess your own thoughts and emotions in terms of changing circumstances. Then, as an individual, you will be able to comprehend the changing landscape and know your place and direction with greater clarity. Similarly, the group or organization must engage in reflexive learning in order to respond proactively to new circumstances and to change to meet new conditions.

It's very interesting that establishing a sense of purpose and direction for all the world to see is something that requires looking inward and challenging yourself – or maybe better, your self. Whether we're talking about an individual or group, there is always a tension between our personal self-image (the way that we think of ourselves) and the way the outside world sees us. Sometimes, perhaps most times, our personal identity lags behind developments in the outside world, and sometimes our identity is out in front. But in either case, it's important to understand the interaction of your identity and the demands of the world around you.

Vision as Direction or Purpose

In leading, you must appeal to both the head and the heart. In contrast to real acts of leadership that appeal to both, most planning processes seek to rationalize the organization's vision through statements of mission and objectives that drain the vision of whatever emotive power it may have held at the outset. Vision dissolves into technique; it fails to energize, and executives fail to lead.

Certainly, a group may be inspired by the beauty and elegance of a grand idea – think "I Have a Dream" – but remember the hours, days, and months of struggle and conversation and, in this case, prayer, that led up to Martin Luther King's speech on the mall in Washington. King had a special capability to draw insight and substance from those he worked with – and from those he worked against. (Indeed, I suspect that he learned as much from the infamous Bull Connor and the KKK as from his own colleagues in the SCLC.)

The "I Have a Dream" speech was an articulation of a narrative that had been growing for years as King engaged others in Montgomery, in Birmingham, across the South, across the nation, and even internationally. The grand idea that King articulated on the mall in Washington was not his alone, but one he heard in the voices of the oppressed in the South (and elsewhere), one he heard as he traveled to India to learn about civil disobedience, and one he heard in the heated national debates on civil rights.

As King demonstrated, your role as a leader is not to create the vision or plan, but to engage with and to learn from others, to help shape their understanding of the world, then to articulate a purpose and direction for the group or organization that is so powerful that it calls people to action.

Ultimately, Kayla and Mike, leadership is not just dreaming, it is the process by which dreams are made real. But is not an easy, nor is it always a rational process. Anyone who leads must recognize the interplay of the objective and intuitive, while at the same time being sensitive to tension between the material and the ideological. You must even recognize that fate or luck sometimes play with you and sometimes play against you.

And, as a practical matter, you must clarify the ideas and commitments that will guide the work of the organization, while at the same time building a capacity for adaptability through reflexive learning. That work, incompletely captured by the simplistic idea of the "vision thing," is really the essence of leadership – to energize!

Yours,

Bob

18
LETTER FROM BOB
January 30

Dear Kayla and Mike,

Let's talk about some of the skills that are needed as we move from the old leadership to the new. For many years, leaders and managers in organizations of all types – business, government, nonprofit, education, and the like – gave special attention to what they called the "hard skills," the technical skills that are required to get the work done. In one case, that might mean skills in construction, in another it might mean skills in accounting, in still another it might mean skills in food preparation. The emphasis on hard skills, however, masked the importance of "people skills," which are also called "process skills," or "soft skills."

Early business education evolved from the idea of apprentices being trained by experts in the field, whether that be making shoes, building homes, educating children, or whatever else. The emphasis was on learning how to create the "outputs" that the field demanded – shoes, homes, educated children. Apprentices learned the hard skills of their disciplines from the masters. Around the beginning of the twentieth century, however, a new dimension was added with the discovery of "management."

Interestingly, it was Frederick Taylor, who is most known for his work on time and motion studies of specific jobs, who also recognized that someone needed to perform those studies (even if informally) and take corrective action in the interest of more efficient production. That became the role of the manager.

Taylor and others considered the primary skills associated with management to be the analysis of data and information concerning the efficiency and productivity of the work being done. Where the hard skills in a bakery may be those needed to create a birthday cake, the hard skills in management, from the beginning, were those of quantitative analysis.

But as the managerial class that characterizes modern organizations grew, people began to recognize that managers needed more than a knowledge of the job, they needed to understand how to effectively interact with other people. They needed people skills, process skills, or "soft skills."

But the hard skills of management continued to dominate. Even today most business administration programs emphasize the hard skills of quantitative and financial analysis, often with limited attention to the people skills required to manage the work. The same orientation is found in public administration (where courses in quantitative policy analysis have displaced courses in public management and organizational behavior), and in nonprofit management, social work, and educational administration as well.

Though the emphasis in these programs is on analytic capabilities, there typically remains at least one course in both the graduate or undergraduate business or public administration curriculum that covers "organizational behavior" or "OB." That course purports to provide a way of thinking and acting more effectively (efficiently?) in working with others.

OB courses usually include such topics as communications, motivation and engagement, decision-making, managing conflict, power and politics, organizational culture and change, creativity and innovation, managing stress, and working in groups and teams. Supporting these skills are such ideas as knowing oneself, understanding perception and attribution, and building self-awareness.

The people skills taught in the OB course are important in all kinds of organizations and are relevant to both management and leadership. While the specific tasks we undertake vary from situation to situation and from time to time, the "soft" skills are always needed. For example, wherever you work, you will be confronted by process issues such as communications and motivation. That holds whether you are managing a department store, a restaurant, or a professional baseball team. The "tasks" – what you are working on at that moment (motivating the sales staff, handling complex catering orders, choosing and announcing a starting lineup, etc.) – come and go, but as long as you are dealing with other people, the process skills will always be there.

I have long thought (and I still do) that developing these skills is quite helpful to people trying to navigate the turbulent waters of groups and organizations. But I'm coming to believe that these skills are most helpful within the particular context of traditional organizations; that is, these skills are the ones that are helpful in our transactions, our interactions based on exchanges of this for that.

These are the skills that Kim learned in her one course in organizational behavior, which you might remember she thought of as "fluffy." But even these skills are not enough when it came to building fully human relationships.

New Skills for Today and Tomorrow

I'm now convinced that organizations of the future will require a dramatic reworking of the skills needed for organizational work. They will require a focus on a new set of relationship skills: empathy, vulnerability, humility, inclusiveness, authenticity, transparency, generosity, balance, patience, learning agility, caring, compassion, and love.

I struggled to find a label for these skills, thinking of various ways to characterize what some might consider "softer than soft." For example, I thought about "soft as the petals of a rose," "soft as a baby's bottom," and even Charmin's phrase, "ultra-soft." But I finally settled on the word "squishy." (I did so for several reasons: "squishy" is not a word that is used a lot in other contexts. I like the alliteration of soft and squishy. And squishy is just a fun word to say – it tickles your mouth! Try it!)

The squishy skills are increasingly referred to as necessary to balance the rational one-sidedness of the traditional soft skills. The squishy skills require emotional intelligence and sensitivity to the needs and interests of others, even when those are not apparent on the surface. They require reading the person or the situation from the inside as well as the outside and from the heart as well as the head.

I realize that these skills might also be called traits, attributes, aspects of personality, qualities, and so on. But I think it's fair, in this context, to think of them as skills or capabilities. I like the term "skills," because it implies that these abilities can be learned and improved upon. They are not just "built-in" aspects of our personality that are unchanging over time, but at least in part skills that can be developed with attention and practice.

Some say that you can't teach what we're calling squishy skills, for example that you can't teach empathy or courage. I would just say that we have not yet learned how to teach the squishy skills. Today, at best, classroom discussions of topics like empathy and courage are devoted to reasons that managers or leaders should adopt these qualities, rather than how they might go about learning them.

For example, to increase skills in interpersonal communications, we have developed approaches to teaching and learning, breaking down communications into teachable skills, such as active listening or supportive communications. On the other hand, we are still developing ways of building our capacity for empathy, transparency, and the like. But there is little doubt that such approaches can be developed over time.

But maybe "teaching" may not even be the right phrasing. Some would say that these skills are natural to the human experience, but that we are taught to suppress and to devalue them. The issue may be in part to find ways to re-access these skills. New studies of the brain have demonstrated that we are wired for some of these skills. It may be that we just need to reconnect and repair the wiring.

I now think of the soft skills as better suited to the transactional exchanges typical of traditional organizations, and the squishy skills as better suited to building the healthy human relationships needed in contemporary and future organizations. For this reason, the soft skills seem to me more related to management and the squishy skills more related to leadership (though both areas need both sets of skills, albeit with a different emphasis.)

But, importantly, the squishy skills are not just useful: they are expressions of yourself as you engage with others. Empathy is not just a technique you can employ: it is a part of your being who you are. It is one basis for building genuine human relationships. It reflects the leader within. And this is something we will continue to explore.

One more point. I see communications as central to the soft skills and empathy as central to the squishy skills. Without communication, the other soft skills lose their potency. Without empathy, the same thing happens to the other squishy skills. Over your lifetime, I suspect you will need both soft and squishy skills, and, among these, most of all, communications and empathy. What's interesting is that we can easily think of how these two ideas might be linked. We might even conclude that the essential "blended" skill of leadership today and into the future will be "empathetic communication," something Kim and Bill were just beginning to explore.

Let's also clarify the language I am using here. Even when researchers began to notice the importance of human or social relations in organizations, the technical skills were still considered most important. Moreover, those with hard skills were successful in disparaging the new human relations movement by labeling those skills as soft. (Someone suggested that the soft skills were given that name by someone who didn't have any.)

I have taken this habit even further by calling for skills that are softer than soft, and I have, with a substantial dose of intentional irony, called them "squishy." By doing so, I certainly don't intend to disparage those skills; indeed, I want to elevate them. In my view, the hardest leadership challenges today are not technical in nature but revolve around human expectations and interactions.

Steve Jobs notwithstanding, I don't consider the leader the one to come forward with technical skills to solve problems. Instead, leaders need soft and squishy skills to deal with people, including very difficult people, to negotiate hard bargains in which the interests of different groups collide, and to guide the group in a purposeful direction. While we may call these skills soft and squishy, they are really the most difficult to master, and the ones we rely on in the most difficult situations. So, when I talk about soft and squishy skills, I can say with confidence: squishy skills are the new hard skills.

One other reminder. Leadership is not and will never be based strictly on a set of skills that you acquire – whether hard, soft, or squishy. While you certainly want to leverage your skills, there is also the matter of the substance and perspective you bring to your leadership – that is, your awareness of social and cultural shifts, your willingness to engage ideas and challenge the ordinary, and the moral and philosophical commitments you are willing to make. But skills play a part, and empathetic communications are an important, even critical skill for you (and me) to develop – for leadership and for life.

Developing Skills

I can sense your reaction to that last sentence: well, how do we develop those skills? And how do they help in energizing a group or organization? (I can sense your reaction, empathetically, in part because I put myself in that sentence as well – and I have the same questions. I can advocate greater empathy, but how do I develop my own capacities for empathetic understanding?)

I'm sure you remember our earlier discussion of how the leader energizes the group. Specifically, we talked about "the leadership moment" and the process of engagement between the potential leader and the group. I suggested that the potential leader first needs "standing" to engage the group or organization, but then undertakes a process of dialogue in which he or she simultaneously discovers, reveals, shapes, recreates, and articulates the group's narrative.

What I'm thinking is that there are two particularly important capabilities that leaders need in this process. One is empathetic communication, which I've just introduced, and to which I'll add "supportive communication." The other is "pattern recognition," an idea I've mentioned before, but which I'll comment on in more detail momentarily. But first, empathy.

Empathy is the ability to sense other people's emotions, coupled with the ability to imagine what someone else might be thinking or feeling. It is being able to walk a mile or more in the shoes of another, even if they don't fit! Communication becomes empathetic when you engage both the cognitive and emotional aspects of another's statements, when you recall your own insights and experiences to understand those of the other person, and when you go beyond what is said "on the surface" to understand things at a deeper level of feeling.

Supportive communication, on the other hand, involves not only the transfer of information and ideas but also is the affirming and validating of another and your relationship with that person. Communication is supportive when you respond in a way that fully respects not only the ideas and thoughts of others, but also their feelings and their emotional state. These, of course, are just definitions. Let's see if I can illustrate how they operate in everyday life.

You can probably remember a time when you greeted someone by saying, "How are you?" and were met with "I'm good." Then you responded by saying, "What's wrong?" Somehow, through empathetic listening you knew that their superficial response concealed a deeper and more significant concern. Empathetic communication suggests that what is being communicated outwardly, either through speech or body language, is just the tip of an iceberg. You must carefully listen to what is being said but also probe beneath the surface to more fully understand where the person or group is coming from.

How can you or I develop greater empathy? Obviously, we can't learn empathy by just reading about it or listening to the many YouTube videos on the topic, though both may help. My recommendation – for you and for me – is to practice empathy every day – that is, to view the ideas and actions of others through an empathetic lens as well as through an objective lens. Remembering to do so actually may be the most difficult part. But maybe a couple of Post-It notes here and there will serve as good reminders.

As I understand it, the term "empathy" was actually first used in trying to understand paintings, or more specifically people depicted in paintings. It strikes me that employing empathy to interpret art is another good way of practicing empathy. This could mean regular trips to the art museum, or it could mean similar ways of engaging with music and literature. Listening consciously and inquisitively to music you enjoy, or simply reading a good book and focusing empathetically on the characters in the book seems to me to be a good way to develop greater empathy.

I suspect that one way that the arts provide an avenue to empathetic understanding is that both empathy and artistic expression depend on images, symbols, and metaphors. The language of both empathy and art is not that of rational conversation; it is instead abstract and elusive, a language better suited to the heart than the head. So, go ahead: see and visualize, listen and fantasize, read and conceptualize, all in the interest of a deeper understanding of human experience.

Empathetic communication is the first step toward meaningful engagement; supportive communication is the second. Supportive communication recognizes that it is your responsibility to comprehend the message that is being transmitted and to add insight and elaboration, but also to enhance relationships within the group or organization.

Imagine that you are in a meeting and one of your employees makes a suggestion for a new account numbering system. You might say, "Seriously? That's the stupidest thing I've ever heard." (Actually, I don't think you would really say that – it's just an illustration!) A better and more supportive alternative might be to say, "That's an interesting suggestion, and I appreciate you bringing it to our attention."

Supportive communication is two-way, not one-way. It builds on what is being said, and it is conjunctive, not disjunctive (meaning each statement directly relates to the one before). Most of all, as in my illustration, supportive communication is validating, not demeaning; it helps all parties to the conversation (the relationship) feel recognized, understood, accepted, and valued.

Empathetic and supportive communications are essential to leadership. Both will help you gain a fuller and more complete understanding of the group's history, its evolution, its current state, and its potential. You may also gain insight into the differences between the group's current direction and the aspirations and potential that lie just beneath the surface. You will then be able to craft and articulate a masterful story that captures the purpose and direction of the group.

Once more, the narrative you construct and articulate may be one of which the group itself is completely unaware. No one person in the group may have previously told the story in quite that way; in fact, probably not. Many people have different pieces of the puzzle that the leader gathers, elaborates, then puts together. The final picture will still have come from the group, though members of the group may not recognize it. (That is why "visions" are often attributed to the leader, even when they are drawn primarily from the group.)

Pattern Recognition

A related capability essential to my sketch of the process of leading is what some call "pattern recognition" – the capacity to listen, to observe, and then to identify connections among ideas and aspirations that are not apparent to others. Pattern recognition is not easy, whether you are talking about patterns in nature, patterns in art and music, or patterns in human thought (as we are here). But it is becoming more familiar.

In machine learning or statistical analysis, pattern recognition focuses on the recognition of regularities in data; in psychology, pattern recognition focuses on identifying related stimuli and connecting information across fields; for our purposes, pattern recognition in leadership is the ability to see order in a somewhat random, even chaotic set of ideas and emotions held by members of a group.

As you engage with others, you will find strands of human meaning that tie together. But finding such patterns among the many voices you hear and ideas you confront is very difficult. Additionally, you will probably find that there is not just one pattern, but many. And you will have to sort out which elements to incorporate into the eventual primary narrative. At the same time, you will have to guard against being drawn to the ideas of those with the greatest power or even those who are the most articulate. Everyone's view is important.

You will have to draw from the many and often complex ideas you encounter so as to articulate the purpose and direction of the group or organization in a way that is at once comprehensive, simple, meaningful, and compelling. You have the responsibility of taking the many ideas expressed in conversations with the group, putting them in the top of the funnel, and allowing just the right combination of words and images to emerge.

In my view, those who lead, more than others, must excel in recognizing and recovering form, sorting out the relevant elements from those that distract, and identifying patterns that others fail to see. The capacity to take many seemingly disconnected ideas and aspirations and put them together in a meaningful pattern is absolutely essential. One hint – the right combination of words and images – is likely to be comprised of elements that are the most emotionally charged. But if you can keep those emotional charges contained and channeled, elements of a consistent narrative, they will be the most effective in energizing the group.

Such notions as empathetic and supportive communication and pattern recognition (especially the latter) rarely find their way into discussions of leadership skills, but given the way we are talking about leading, they are central. I do think they can be broken down into their components and learned in the same way we learn other soft or squishy skills. In fact, as you explore different leadership development programs you might ask which ones include these elements of practice. However, don't expect them to use the term "squishy skills." That's just among us.

Yours,

Bob

19

LETTER FROM KAYLA

February 2

Dr. Bob

Wow! That's a lot to react to!

I'm not sure I'll have time to go through all the notes that I made in the margins of your last few letters. Many were question marks, some were alternative wordings, and many were exclamation marks or the word, "YES," written in large bold letters in the margin.

I texted Mike after receiving your letters. What was remarkable to both of us was how changing the basic definition of "leading" or "leadership," opened new ways of thinking about these other issues. We agreed that, rather than debate the details of your letters, it might be most helpful for us to tie some of these issues to our own experiences. So that's what I'm going to try to do. And Mike will do the same.

The first two of this set of letters focused on the importance of transactions versus relationships. I can certainly understand how, at least in the abstract, traditional organizations appear to be based on transactions. In my organizational sociology course, we talked about "the rational model of organization," one that assumes that a goal is being pursued and everything else is an attempt to order human and other resources so that the utmost efficiency is obtained. (I probably should footnote that, but I think we agreed not to do footnotes.) Thinking in this way does indeed make the organization seem like a series of exchanges or transactions.

I recall that one author talked about an "inducements/contributions" formula. By that he meant that organizations are built on offering inducements such as money, power, or prestige in order to receive contributions such as basic labor, commitment to the purpose of the organization, and loyalty.

(Hey, do I sound like an academic or what?)

Our organization offers such inducements. My biweekly paycheck is, of course, a reflection of that idea. It's one of my inducements to contribute, though money is not the only one. There are many others, such as having a pleasant place to work, doing meaningful work, being with supportive people, etc. Similarly, the consulting work that I do with any state or local agency is covered under a contract in which each party establishes what they will provide the other, and expect to be provided in return. It's a transaction or an exchange.

But I wouldn't say that everything that happens in my organization is transactional. We do have relationships with one another that go beyond formal exchanges. (I think these patterns of relationships used to be called the "informal" organization. Again, footnote the organizational sociology class.) We build personal relationships with others in the organization, both up and down and sideways. For example, I think of our CEO as not only the big boss of our company but also as a friend who cares about me and supports me. And I respect him.

I suppose you could say that there's a transaction there with his support prompting my respect, but that seems like a pretty cold way of describing a personal relationship. I would say today's young employees, including the dreaded millennials (HA!), place more value on relationships than previous generations. Maybe for that reason, organizations are starting to emphasize relationships rather than transactions. I wonder whether you think that each new generation subtly reshapes organizations so that they are consistent with the values of that new generation? That would be interesting to explore, wouldn't it?

I liked your story about your (former) neighbor Kim. Her experience certainly showed the importance of relationships. I guess Kim learned an important lesson and maybe I'm learning that same lesson. But I think both Kim and I are operating in a period of transition, a shift from one set of organizational values to another, from transactions to relationships, and if one person bases his or her work on transactions and the other on relationships (or vice versa), there will be confusion and conflict. My question, then, is: how can we resolve this issue and move toward making relationships more central to our work?

The next letter, the one on vision, was a little easier to deal with. I've been involved in some strategic planning exercises already in our company, and I've seen them fail and wind up on a shelf in the storage closet, just as you said. Still, my management classes placed a strong emphasis on strategy and strategic planning. That makes me wonder whether strategy is more associated with management, and vision (or direction or purpose) is more associated with leading. That makes sense to me.

I do think that discussing the goals of the organization along with careful analysis of strengths, weaknesses. opportunities, and threats is a healthy thing for people throughout the organization to do. But, as you say, when you start making predictions of what you should or can accomplish in five or ten years, and then base your objectives on those predictions, you wind up with something that is going to become irrelevant very quickly.

Finally, your discussion of soft versus squishy skills made a lot of sense to me – though I have to admit I had never really thought about skills in this way. (Do you really want to call them "squishy"?) And I guess I would question whether the squishy skills are in fact skills, or whether instead they should be called "qualities." But I'm not sure that really matters.

What does matter is that these squishy skills are increasingly being identified as very important, both by academics and those of us in the real world. The term "empathy," for example, seems to come up on almost a daily basis in our firm, certainly in the articles that Robert suggest that we read. (Yes, he sometimes gives us homework assignments!)

In our case, he means that we need to empathetically understand and support each other and do the same with our clients. Again, like the transaction and relationships thing, this new reliance on empathy may go a little too far. Aren't there limits?

I also wonder how you can teach the squishy skills. As you said, the organizational behavior textbook that we used was basically organized around the soft skills. It would be interesting to see a book written from the perspective of the squishy skills. Maybe you have some thoughts about this – or maybe you are already writing that book!

So, that's all for now. I look forward to your next letters!

Kayla

20
LETTER FROM MIKE
February 12

Bob

Kayla said she was going to write you to let you know that she and I decided to focus our responses to your recent letters around the applicability of your ideas to our work situations. If you haven't seen her letter yet, you might wait to read this one until after reading hers. I think it would make a little more sense.

Your letters on relationships really struck home to me. Like Kim in your letters, I once got burned by my failure to maintain strong relationships with others in the company. I had been selected to attend a two-week professional development program at the Duke University. During those two weeks, we learned a variety of new financial management techniques that we could implement almost immediately upon my returning home.

And that's just what I did. For the next month following the program I not only helped implement the systems in my own division, but spent a great deal of my time out of town on assignment to rework some of the financial management systems elsewhere in our company, using the ideas and techniques I had learned at Duke. So, I was essentially away from my normal workgroup for about six weeks.

When I finally returned, many of the folks around me seemed to have almost forgotten who I was. Some even seemed a little hostile – they said I was just sucking up to the boss, making the modest mistakes that we had been making into big deals, and no longer caring about the most important thing in our organization – the office softball team.

The team had been formed by the human resources officer in our group and had played in a highly competitive fast pitch softball division. Some had joked that the HR director had recruited me as much for my talent on the baseball field as for my work-related skills. I was a pretty good hitter and did a decent job at shortstop, a position they desperately needed to have filled. But the six weeks I was away was during the core of the softball season, so I was basically out for the year. The comments from my teammates when I got back reflected their disappointment with me.

I now think the comments that I took so seriously at the time were mostly joking, but I'm sure that my relationship coefficient declined considerably over that six-week period. I hadn't really tried to cultivate these relationships: they just happened. But these people were available to me to call on in places where I needed a little help. It occurred to me that, if I really tried to develop relationships, I would probably have more places to go – and I would have more friends that could help me along the way with the personal stuff. I count this as a missed opportunity, and have tried to correct for it ever since.

Your comments on vision and strategic planning were more difficult for me. My current organization is one that is focused on data analytics. For us, thinking about strengths and weaknesses, etc. makes a lot of sense. We rely on careful analysis of markets and insurance for almost everything we do. To talk about empathy and emotion in the planning process is a little strange given our company's need to focus on what is objectively correct.

I guess I can understand how the other approach would work in, say, a human resources or social services organization, but in the kind of work that I do, objectivity and precision are very important. How could we account for the deviations that feelings and emotions inevitably bring about?

What's curious is that, even as I say these things, I find myself attracted to the more subjective, intuitive, emotional side of things. But the job that I'm in requires all the opposites. And I seem to be doing well in that world.

I remember that, in class, you talked about personality types based on the work of a Swiss psychologist, whose name has slipped away. As I remember, part of his deal was to talk about how different people come to favor different personality characteristics, and how those occasionally come into conflict with one another. But you also said that each of us has access to all the characteristics, depending on the situation that we are in. For example, one person could have a preference for a more creative and intuitive approach to the world, but if they find themselves in a situation requiring the opposites, that is, a more analytical and data-driven approach, they can adapt to what that situation requires.

A couple weeks ago, I decided to try to observe different personality types in the organization, selecting one person to "analyze" each week. My first case involved a woman named Mary Ellen, someone who I thought of as emotionally "highly strung." She proved to be the perfect case. In my dealings with Mary Ellen, I often came away from conversations thinking that "she just doesn't get it," meaning she just doesn't fit in with the way we do our business. But as I more carefully considered Mary Ellen, trying to put myself in her position (in her personality?), I wondered whether I was the one who didn't "get it." She seemed to be true to herself, comfortable in her different perspective, but recognizing that her natural tendencies, especially her creativity, didn't fit the role that she was in. I wonder if that was related to her emotional "tightness."

I also wondered if this was the same situation that I find myself in. I seem to adapt well to the rational and analytic world in which we work, but I'm not completely comfortable with that. I sometimes feel more at home when I'm working on creative projects outside work, and spending my time with people I enjoy, not just for their capabilities and what they can do, but for who they are. Am I schizophrenic? Or at least conflicted? How can I find my true self – and create a life that reflects that true self?

Obviously, this is something I need to work on and I'd certainly appreciate your comments.

Mike

21
LETTER FROM BOB
February 20

Dear Kayla and Mike,

What thoughtful letters you both wrote! I really appreciate your taking the time to study my comments on transactions versus relationships, vision versus purpose and direction, and soft versus squishy skills, and to provide such insightful critiques and suggestions. Let me try to respond to some of your main points.

Kayla, I enjoyed the way you drew on your background in sociology, especially organizational sociology, to connect some of our thoughts about transactions and relationships to earlier writing in organization theory. You are correct – the "inducements/contributions" formulation is the epitome of what we have called "transactional organization." The idea was that individual decisions (transactions) about whether to stay in the organization or whether to contribute one's labor from day to day resulted from rational (or nearly rational) decisions about whether the exchange was worthwhile to both parties.

You are also correct in tying some of my comments on relationships to the notion of informal organizations. And, again drawing on your sociology course, you probably could have continued to trace more relationship-oriented approaches to organization through the development of organizational humanism and on to some contemporary ideas about "Presence" and even "Theory U," just to pick a couple of random examples.

That brings us to the specific question you asked about new generations influencing the values of leadership in organizations. I do think that the general culture in which we live influences our ideas about leadership in these settings. And I'd even go so far as to say that the sub-cultures, even micro-cultures of particular groups or locations, affect what's expected of leadership there.

So, yes, I would agree that each new generation demands a rethinking of leadership, one in line with their own values and preferences. I even think that occurs without any conscious effort to make changes. But my challenge to you goes beyond the changes that your generation will naturally bring about. Imagine the changes that could be made if you were fully and personally committed to reorder the world of leadership. That's exactly the challenge that I'm posing for you – to move our notion of leadership beyond its current boundaries and even beyond the natural shifts that accompany a change in generations. I want you to create a new leadership for a new generation.

Moving on: you have always been two of the smartest people in the room, but now you find yourself in rooms where smart alone is not rewarded. Here, smart must now be combined with sensitive. I'd be interested in your response, of course, but I think that you are both beginning to open yourselves to the interplay of the rational and the intuitive. I'll be eager to see how that develops.

Mike, I was particularly interested in your comments on finding your "true self." (That phrase sounds a little ambitious to me, but I think I know what you mean.) The work you're talking about comes from Carl Jung. Jung talked about the differences in personality types, something that has been taken up by various groups, each parading their own instruments and interpretations (MBTI, etc.). Unfortunately, this can lead to excessive "labeling," separating people into named groups. (At some meetings, people are even asked to wear name tags or even hats, that label them as one type or another.)

But Jung's main point was that the only reason for talking about the differences was to provide a basis for integrating the personality, that is bringing together all the capabilities that the individual has, a process he called "individuation." Instead of splitting apart aspects of our individual personalities, Jung was more concerned with integrating our personhood. Instead of dividing people, he was more interested in bringing people together.

I think you're right on track to employ this material, but remember that what is most important is to integrate all aspects of your personality. That first requires identifying the different aspects, including what your strengths are, and what your weaknesses are, but that's just a first step toward individuation. And, I suspect that's really what your quest was all about: how you might emerge into the next part of your life with a balance or even integration of the various strengths that you bring.

Finally, in both your letters, your reactions to my comments about replacing transactions with relationships was very interesting. I think you're right. As long as the bottom line in organizations is described in economic terms, the use of transactions will seem appropriate. I also agree with your suggestion that there are certain skills or qualities needed for transactions, and a different set of skills needed for relationships – soft and squishy? But on this point, maybe I should follow Jung's model, and say that we need to identify, maybe even balance different skills, but ultimately – and this is probably in the far different future – to integrate hard, soft, and squishy.

Again, thanks for your wonderful comments and for the material you shared. But having said all that, let me see if I can move the conversation forward in a different way.

Evolving Leadership – A Summary

First I want to review and summarize the ideas that we have developed to this point with respect to the personal nature of leadership. Then we will turn to some of the broader issues that we need to address, including the most difficult, the role of power in leadership.

As we have discussed, the term leadership has evolved in curious ways over the course of history, but it has almost always been in part about leaders exciting others and in part about leaders controlling others. It has been about vision and encouragement, but it has also been very much about power and position.

For centuries, indeed millennia, leadership (originally rulership) was defined by power and the roles it established – the ruler and the ruled, masters and slaves, bosses and subordinates, managers and the managed. Skip way ahead, and we'll see that we have largely continued to lead with power, but we have also extended the notion of hierarchy, allowing the growth of organizations of massive size and global reach. Even more recently, we have added advanced technology to the mix, bringing instantaneous worldwide communication, a redistribution of information, and much more.

The result has been that when most people think of a leader today, they think of someone who holds a significant position in business, government, or the third or nonprofit sector. Leadership has been redefined as the work of the top manager or executive. The person at the top is called the leader. His or her work, though called "leadership," is mostly the work of executive management. Leadership has been narrowed to minimize its role both in developing an agenda for action, what we might call "aspiration," and in encouraging people to follow that path, what we might call "inspiration."

Leaders, in this standard view, are the ones who accomplish the goals of their communities, their corporations, and their countries. They are the ones that get results. And they get results typically by managing organizations through variations on traditional hierarchical structures and practices.

This is the key point. If leaders are defined as executive managers, the kinds of activities they can and will engage in will be confined by the expectations of traditional management. Internally, they will largely operate from the top down through hierarchical structures. They will employ a transactional approach to the organization and hire, fire, and promote, based on the skills that are appropriate to that approach, largely what we call soft skills. Externally, they will be expected to scan the organization's environment, looking for opportunities and anticipating changes, negotiate with stakeholders and other groups, and establish a vision and associated practices to better position the organization.

In contrast to the current tendency to equate leadership with executive management, in these letters, we have explored new ways of defining leadership and the expectations that we might have of leaders, following a different understanding of their role. We have defined leadership more broadly to embrace a wide variety of activities that are not constrained by the expectations of hierarchy. Leading, in this view, can happen in many contexts, ranging from the child on the playground to the adult in the boardroom.

We have especially focused on the development of genuine human relationships and the development of what we have called "squishy skills," both aimed at advancing the purpose and direction of the group or organization.

In my view, leadership is not simply an objective role to be executed but is a personal experience through which the individual's own growth and development is as important as the impact the person has on the productive process. A major part of understanding leadership is understanding what's inside of us.

Anticipating New Organizations

We have already discussed some of the changes we expect to see in leadership over the coming years, and we will detail these as we proceed. Now I'd like to suggest some changes that I think will occur in organizations over the coming years. I must admit, however, that there is a thin line between what I will predict and what I might hope for, and an equally thin line between what I might hope for and what I think will be necessary for our survival. (You'll also have to forgive me for presenting a numbered list. At least there are no "secrets"!)

1) We are moving from organizations that are highly structured to organizations that will appear to be unstructured, even chaotic. We are accustomed to organizations that look and act like those pictured in the traditional organization chart – highly regimented, slow to innovate, and resistant to change. These are organizations that excel in delivering hundreds or thousands of products that are exactly alike (or with only cosmetic differences). But today and into the future, we are likely to see more organizations, or ways of working together, that are open and free-flowing, flexible, creative, and adept at change. The agility of these organizations and their leaders will be paramount.

2) We are moving from organizations that produce a single product or service over and over to organizations that have the capacity to shift quickly from product to product, service to service, or experience to experience. The industrial assembly line model is not dead (and we still need its products), but it is increasingly being shifted from human hands to technical, even robotic hands. From here on, the most successful organizations will be those that have developed a human capacity for creativity, change, and innovation. It's not just more of the same: it's more and differentiated outcomes. In this world, personalization will become a key. Those organizations that can

deliver goods, services, and experiences tailored to the individual will have a great advantage. We are moving from organizations that distribute authority and power in a top-down fashion to organizations that depend much more on "autonomous collaboration." Top-down is dying. The term "boss" is obsolete. Even the term "manager" is being called into question by those who rebel against the idea of major portions of their lives being managed by others.

3) In the future, individuals are less likely to be "told" to collaborate, but more likely to come together as individuals – by choice – to make things happen. People will be offered the chance to design their own jobs and select those with whom they work. And they will be able to change the conditions of work quickly, depending on the flow of both internal and external demands. Closely related to this point, we are moving from organizations that assign people to certain tasks to organizations that give individuals a much greater role in defining their contributions, allowing them to focus on work that is meaningful to them. In the past and still today, organizations were designed "from the top," largely to achieve a division of labor and a hierarchical pattern of power and authority. But imagine a future in which ways of working together arise spontaneously and organically from the bottom up, the top down, or anywhere in between, based on individuals recognizing that certain things need to happen, and through their autonomous involvement, taking meaningful action on their own. The way in which individual purpose pushes organizational purpose (as opposed to the other way around) will become a larger issue, just as the quest for meaningful experiences will become more important.

4) We are moving (very slowly) from organizations that place a primary emphasis on financial measures of success to those that consider public value and sustainability paramount. Both public and private organizations today operate against a financial bottom line, defined by what the public is willing to pay, either in taxes or corporate profits. Though organizations of all types – public, private, nonprofit – claim to operate in the public interest, that interest is often buried beneath the drive for efficiency and productivity, both modern-day extrapolations of "the bottom line." The alternative is to focus on the social and environmental systems that sustain us. The results of our not doing so are evident all around us – war, famine, and terrorism threatening individual lives, to say nothing of climate change and nuclear warfare threatening the entire planet. But the movement toward corporate social responsibility and its offshoots hints that a different direction may be possible – though exceptionally difficult.

5) We are (hopefully) moving from organizations that model severe income inequality to those that model a more equitable distribution of resources, both within the organization and between the organization and its clients or customers. There is a peculiar incentive system that underlies our current

model of organization – the assumption that individuals act in their self-interest and that self-interest makes the system work. For example, to reach the higher and more highly paid positions, you must succeed at the lower levels, and that increases productivity. But the inevitable consequences of structuring organizations based on self-interest (which too easily translates into greed) are severe power differences and income inequality. (While income inequality has received the most public attention, the differences in power between the top and the bottom are just as extreme.) In any case, at some point power and income inequality may lead to a complete breakdown of organizational systems based on self-interest, and that will mean either the total collapse or a complete transformation of today's organizations.

In any case, we might say that we are moving from traditional organizations to a completely different way of getting things done – a way that features less structured, less power-oriented, more relationship-oriented, and more sustainable organizations. Maybe we are moving from organizations to collaborations. Or facilitations. Or harmonizations. Or perhaps simply new ways of working together.

The More Things Change

Throughout all the changes that we have forecast, there is one consistent theme – we are moving from a system based on power and control to one emphasizing autonomy and choice. The only real questions are how the move will be ignited and how long it will take. As you point out, we have a long way to go to even balance the rational and the intuitive/emotive in leadership.

But someday, maybe 100 years from now, we may well have organizations that are as strong in the intuitive/emotive realm as today's organizations are strong in the rational. That's obviously a prediction that I can't substantiate. But any balanced assessment of the direction and pull of social forces and social energy today would suggest that's likely to happen.

Just one more sidebar. I no longer think that the direction of social change or the path of social energies can be explained or predicted in rational terms. You can't make rational predictions about the human experience, because that experience is not solely rational. To grasp the unfolding of the human experience, you must get in touch with the irrational, the emotional, and the intuitive as well. They all must be considered as we think about how our experiences provide us insight into the historical evolution of freedom and autonomy. (Here I'm using the term "history" not as a record of past events, but as the path or trajectory of human life, past, present, and future.)

Many philosophers have hypothesized such a trend toward greater autonomy in our work in organizations and in our lives generally. G. W. F. Hegel, for example, suggested that history is the unfolding of reason and, in turn, the advance of autonomy and freedom. Other social theorists have suggested that social theory provides an avenue to explore this alternative future. Herbert Marcuse writes, "Social theory is supposed to analyze existing societies . . . to identify demonstrable tendencies (if any) which might lead beyond the existing state of affairs." It may also be able to determine the basic institutional changes which are the prerequisites for the transition to a higher stage of development: "'higher' in the sense of a more rational and equitable use of resources, minimization of destructive conflicts, and enlargement of the realm of freedom." Continuing the same theme, one of the most significant social theorists of modern times, Jürgen Habermas, describes the advance of society toward greater autonomy as a move toward "emancipation, individuation, and communications free of domination."

More sophisticated language, I suppose, but it just supports the idea that we are moving toward more human connections or relationships and, at the same time, a greater sense of autonomy and choice.

Yours,

Bob

22
LETTER FROM KAYLA
February 25

Dr. Bob

It really was helpful of you to summarize what we've been talking about. I especially liked the way you expressed our skepticism about organizational life today. I've heard various critiques of bureaucracy over the years, critiques that have taken aim at the instrumental nature of organizations, their dehumanizing effects on employees and clients, and their inherent bias in favor of the status quo. (I'm becoming a sociologist again!)

I've also heard concerns about specific organizations; the environmental damage caused by Exxon, the ethical failings of Enron, and the blatant efforts to undermine safety regulations by Volkswagen, etc.

But, you are saying that, beyond the product of any single organization, the current organizational model leads to negative outcomes. You're arguing that the failure of organizations to include sustainability as part of their mission has impacted climate change. You're also saying that the incentive system of most major organizations leads directly to income inequality. You were careful to point out the positive outcomes that organizations have produced. But you also explored how certain features of organizational life inevitably produce negative consequences.

These are pretty broad charges, but not inconsistent with what I have read and witnessed over the years. I have a couple of reactions. First, I can't remember anything in my management courses that came close to these concerns, except for some discussions of the "triple bottom line" in a strategy course, and a discussion of ethical behavior in the course on business ethics. But even there, the discussions were framed in terms of productivity; that is, if you're not attentive to ethical and environmental concerns, you may lose business. Unethical behavior can cost you dearly, not only in terms of reputation, but in terms of dollars. In any case, these discussions seem to be geared toward particular managers or particular organizations, rather than being an indictment of the basic, underlying characteristics of traditional organizations.

Second, you didn't specifically mention how power and control affect our current thinking about organization, but surely power is an issue that we find confusing in all organizations, and a characteristic that has negative consequences, both internally and externally. I'd be very interested in what you have to say about power.

And, speaking of power, remember you promised to discuss the roadblocks to leadership faced by young women today.

Meanwhile, at the company, we rarely talk about some of the ideas that our letters have addressed. We just take these things for granted. They are part of the established platform from which we work. But that way of doing things often leads to frustration, resentment, and poor performance. But again, it all is very subtle – "hidden."

For example, I don't see Robert as the nasty, top-down, "everything is about power," boss that seems to be the villain in some of the critiques of organizations. He's much more relaxed than that. But I suppose when push comes to shove, he could turn on his power, as easily as he now turns on his charm. (I hope you won't show that directly to him – it's really not an indictment of one person and more an indictment of the system – but it could be taken the other way.)

I want to turn to what's happening to me. While I've been engaged in these discussions of leadership with you and Mike, my work has progressed in a steady fashion. I'm trying to establish relationships with people all around the organization and I'm trying to think about experiences that would be helpful to me in learning more about leadership. There was a little rumor floating around that I was going to be considered for a key role if a new contract with a local government is confirmed. But that will be a while, if it ever even happens.

I'll let you know.

Kayla

23
LETTER FROM MIKE
February 27

Bob

Just when I thought I was going to settle back into my current position, I was contacted by a local nonprofit that provides a wide variety of services to several traditionally underserved neighborhoods, everything from health care to affordable housing to job training. They want me to be their executive director, or at least they have contacted me to measure my interest!

At first, I just moved the email to my "Forget it" file – and forgot it. But that evening I mentioned it to Annie and was a little surprised that she seemed quite interested in learning the details. I thought she was just reacting to the fact that we wouldn't have to move. But as we talked I realized she was echoing things I have been saying for a while. You may remember that in my very first note to you I talked about seeking new sources of meaning in my life and work. I have continued to feel that way and have taken some comfort in your calm and relaxed attitude toward this. Maybe this is the opportunity I've been hoping for!

Since then I have reviewed the material that they sent to me, I've talked with the current chief executive about the operation, and I've submitted a formal application. I don't know this will go anywhere, but I'm getting excited about it! On the other hand, I'm trying not to go overboard, especially because I realize my background is about as far from social work and healthcare as it could be. I'm not the ideal candidate, I suppose, but I guess we'll leave that up to them. I'll let you know more as I find out more.

Oh yes, I've been waiting for your take on power in leadership and organization. I sense it's coming!

Mike

24

LETTER FROM BOB

March 8

Dear Kayla and Mike,

Kayla and Mike, you have asked a couple of times where power fits into all of this. Kayla, you asked about women and power and, Mike, you sensed correctly that a discussion was on the way. Let me address these concerns in this and the next two letters.

First let me comment on how I react to power in leadership and management. To give away the answer before the explanation, I would say "Not well!"

Let me tell you why. I have described two kinds of leadership: one I have called "old," and the other I have called "new." (How clever!) Associated with these, we have talked about two approaches to organization, one I have called "old," the other I have called "new." (Once more, very clever. I'm on a roll!) Remember that the differences between old and new are not just a matter of time passing. Instead, the old and the new models differ in terms of the types of human interaction that underlie each set. In both these models, the way that power is handled is critical.

So, let's get started. I have always found power to be among the most troublesome concepts in leadership and management. Power cuts in many directions. Some find themselves drawn to power; others are repelled by it. Some value what power can do for them; others fear what it can do to them.

As I said early on, many people equate leadership with power. Others, and I would put myself in this group, think that the exercise of power signals a failure of leadership. If you have to resort to power, you're not energizing – you are not leading. You are controlling, directing, forcing, coercing, manipulating – whatever you wish – but you are not leading.

Let's think once more about the evolution of power and leadership. From the earliest times, power was central to understanding life in families, in work, and in politics. Power meant strength, often supported by violence. Even the noted philosopher Aristotle used the physical strength of the male (assumed to translate as well into intellectual strength) as justifying the male's dominant role in the family in ancient Greece.

Similarly, in the world of work, power was a central dynamic. Consider, for example, the master – slave relationship of 2,000 years ago, again justified by Aristotle based on the master's supposed natural and expected position of power. And, of course, in politics and government, from that period to the present, the surest rulers were and are those with superior military forces at their disposal. (Isn't it interesting to think how these ancient practices and their intellectual justifications are reflected in our world even today?)

Over the centuries, power continued to be central to political and economic life. Indeed, most definitions of politics still focus on activities involved in gaining and holding power, especially the power to determine how values are allocated. Power was and is central to other social institutions as well, enshrined in the hierarchy of the Church and the Divine Right of Kings.

Later, with the Industrial Revolution, power and its cousin "authority," which I think of as simply ritualized power, became guiding principles in work organizations of all types, including in government bureaucracy, and especially in the modern Corporation. (In a quirk of technology, as I was writing the previous paragraph, I capitalized the word Church, but then, without my instruction, my dictation software capitalized the word Corporation. How ironic that technology would recognize the apparent relatedness of those two institutions in writing about power.)

A New Look at Power

Leadership continues today to be tied to power. Recently, Jeffrey Pfeffer, a professor at a well-regarded business school, wrote a book arguing that the high-minded interpretation of leadership, which recommends that leaders adopt such characteristics as authenticity, humility, and transparency (as I do) is simply wrong. In contrast, he says, if you look at the actual behavior of successful leaders in business (and presumably elsewhere), a significant number are narcissistic, manipulative, lying, unethical, and overly demanding. His book is not a polemic aimed at reforming the highest offices in corporate America but is a compilation of detailed studies about what matters for success in business today.

This description of corporate leadership is not pretty, but I actually think it's a welcome addition to the literature on leadership. Just think about it. If this is what our current model of leadership and management has brought about, this is simply one more compelling reason to drastically rethink what we mean by leading, and what we expect of our leaders.

As we have seen, our traditional approach to leadership in organizations has led to damage to the environment, income inequality, and limitations on genuine human relationships. In addition, we now see that approach apparently has also created a generation of leaders that, according to Pfeffer, includes power-hungry liars, cheaters, and thieves. There is no question – we operate today under a concept of leadership that is fundamentally flawed.

But despite its flaws, it is pervasive. Our understanding of leadership as based in power and executed through management control has so penetrated every aspect of our culture that it's hard to recognize the possibility of an alternative.

Consider once again the incentive systems of most large organizations. The one who succeeds in getting to the top, the leader, is given more money, more power, and more prestige. So, ambition is often another word for seeking power.

The role of ambition in seeking a position of leadership has several important implications for leaders. Many leaders, being driven by personal ambition, are propelled by ego on the way to the top and exhibit excessive ego when they get there.

While self-confidence is necessary to leadership, as we said before, there's a fine line between confidence and excessive ego. And, of course, history is replete with leaders who have crossed that line. These leaders acted in a heavy-handed, personally demanding manner, which has been questioned in the past but will be strictly off-limits in the future. The cruel and uncaring bosses who screamed at their employees and otherwise abused them in public or private were once thought to be demonstrating passion for their work. Today, such managers are considered relics of the past at best and "toxic" at worst. In the future, they will be considered totally ineffective if not unstable.

Another effect of allowing ambition to spawn excessive ego is the leader's assumption that he or she stands above the rules that apply to everyone else and, indeed, even above the law. In some recent and highly public cases, executives made decisions to break the law, either for personal benefit or to avoid public ridicule for their mistakes. They simply assumed, without thinking things through, that they were immune from the obligations and responsibilities others would take for granted.

Hang on, folks, it gets worse. What I call "power-as-coercion" is based on the belief (at least by those in power) that some persons are superior to others in judgment and resources, and that those people have a right (or even an obligation) to control the behavior of others. At a minimum, these superiors – whom in politics we call presidents, governors, mayors, and so on, and in corporations we call CEOs, executives, managers, and the like – are expected to map out the plan or strategy for the group, then exercise their power or employ incentives to direct their subordinates toward the achievement of their goals.

Moreover, those with power usually try to maintain their position, which, of course, limits the opportunities of others. This is not to say that no one moves from the lowest position to the highest, but such stories are rare – indeed noteworthy because they are so rare.

In any case, power-as-coercion limits the opportunity for people to pursue their life goals without undue constraints. Being subject to the rule of others means that people become locked into structures that primarily benefit those above them in the hierarchy. These "subordinates" are not encouraged to pursue their own goals and ambitions, their own ideas of happiness. The opportunities for subordinates to develop their greatest potential are few, as their paths are laid out before them as "acceptable careers."

The idea of freedom, of course, means that the preferences of the individual are given substantial weight vis-à-vis the collective. That doesn't mean that individuals can do whatever they want: they are constrained by laws and other rules that prohibit acts that violate the rights of others. But the emphasis is on freedom of choice and freedom of action. In contrast, power-as-coercion in groups and organizations acts to limit individual choice to avenues approved by those in positions of power, presumably avenues that will lead to benefits for the organizations (and likely as well for those in positions of power).

What about ethical constraints on the use of power? My own view is that the use of coercive power in leadership or management is always ethically questionable. In addition to the issue of whether power is used for good or evil, power encourages those at the top to do things they would not otherwise do. They cross the lines between influence and persuasion, on one hand, and coercion and, putting it generously, manipulation, on the other. Both strike me as diminishing the coerced person's freedom and independence and amount to a violation of basic individual rights.

Let me be clear. There may be cases in which power, even violence, can be justified. For example, there is the question of whether the use of power and violence is necessary in limiting violations of the social order, as in controlling criminal activity or suppressing others who act with violence. I'll leave that to others to resolve. I'm more concerned, of course, with the dynamics of leadership and management as they are played out between and among individuals.

What's Wrong with a Little Coercion from Time to Time?

You will, of course, recall our description of the leadership moment in earlier letters. That moment is preceded by an open engagement between the potential leader and the group. That dialogue ultimately results in the leader articulating the purpose and direction of the group or organization. I think power-as-coercion interferes with this process in two ways.

First, power-as-coercion sets up an inevitable win – lose contest between those with power and those without (or those with more power and those with less). Transactions based on a contest for power and the resources that support power lead inevitably toward a zero-sum game in which competition is a far more natural approach than cooperation. (Again, I'm not so concerned with whether you say that resources support power or power attracts resources. It doesn't matter whether fried chicken or the fried egg came first, they are inevitably tied to one another.)

Second, power-as-coercion distorts communications and inevitably limits cooperation and collaboration. We have already seen how this works. In speaking to someone in power, you shape your language to defer to that power, you distort the truth ever so slightly (though sometimes quite blatantly). Since traditional organizations are permeated with power, the accumulation of miscommunications caused by the presence of power-as-coercion can be devastating.

Again, all organizations claim that they have communications problems. But these are not just problems in active listening, or the lack of newsletters, etc. They are problems more deeply entwined in the structure of power in the organization. The pervasiveness of power makes it almost impossible for traditional organizations to operate with clarity of purpose, direction, and execution. And without clarity, there are inherent limits on what organizations can do – and what leaders can do.

Power-as-coercion continues a questionable moral tradition, in which power, manipulation, and related tactics allow "superiors" to control the actions of subordinates, limiting their individuality and their freedom to pursue their own purposes. Moreover, power-as-coercion limits the capacity for open communication that is key to new and evolving forms of leadership. It also works against both individual autonomy, on the one hand, and collaborative action (freely entered into), on the other.

In my view, the old leadership, the one that equates leadership with executive management, cannot be separated from coercive power. But as new patterns or new relationships develop, it may well be that management itself will fade away. As we have said, people don't like to be managed or "bossed around." The trick will be to develop ways of implementation or execution that don't rely on power as the motivational force. My guess is that, over a very long term, the motivational forces in an increasing number of organizations will be the individual's desire for meaningful, satisfying, and creative work, taking place in healthy groups and organizations that express community-oriented purposes and directions.

Certainly, in the new leadership, power-as-coercion will be largely irrelevant. The new leadership is not aimed at control or domination. It is instead aimed at energizing. Those seeking to energize others will find coercive power a roadblock; they will find that it gets in the way. Quite frankly, again, Kayla and Mike, if you have to resort to power, you have failed in leadership. On the other hand, the new leadership – dependent not on coercive power, but on relationships, communications, and engagement – will ignite energy and enthusiasm.

I'm guessing that you are wondering at this moment what damaging experiences I had as a child that led me to dislike power so much! But you may also be wondering how the relationship between power and leadership will play out over the coming years. I'll pass on answering the first question, but tackle the second next, by describing an alternative to power-as-coercion, what I will call power-as-capacity.

Yours,

Bob

25
LETTER FROM BOB
April 2

Dear Kayla and Mike,

You may respond to my last letter by calling these thoughts idealistic or out of touch. But there is no reason we shouldn't seek the ideal, even if it proves difficult to attain.

If the direction of social change continues as we expect, we will be challenged to seek organizational patterns and concomitant leadership perspectives that will value autonomy and collaboration. Again, I don't think that possibility is anywhere near being fulfilled, but I do think the movement toward greater autonomy is clear. This idea has implications for our work lives – and for our personal lives as well. A meaningful life is one that expands opportunities for freedom and autonomy. Building a new kind of leadership is a meaningful purpose, perhaps even a calling.

Power-as-Coercion vs. Power-as-Capacity

To this point, I have been using "power" and "power-as-coercion" interchangeably. But power comes in another variety, what I will call "power-as-capacity." In this letter, I want to draw a careful and important distinction between power-as-coercion and power-as-capacity. Specifically, my concerns about power, which I have already noted, relate to power-as-coercion. On the other hand, I see power-as-capacity – that is, personal or community power expressing presence and engagement – as critical to the new leadership.

Power-as-coercion refers to patterns of domination, control, manipulation, status, or rewards/punishments through which one person or one group is able to get another person or group to carry out their wishes. Power-as-coercion in groups and organizations is typically top down, uncompromising, and enforceable. It is expressed in sentences such as the following: "He's the one with the power in this organization," or "She has the power to enforce that rule at any time and in any circumstance."

Power-as-capacity is quite different. At the individual level, power-as-capacity expresses a person's presence, his or her inner strength and ability, depth of character, and moral integrity. At the group level, it refers to the capability an organization, community, or society has to come together to accomplish needed changes. An example might be to say: "She had the power and resilience to complete school, despite working full time and raising two children." You might also say, "They constitute a powerful and strongly linked community." (You'll both remember Armando from one of our classes, who exuded such calm self-confidence – or presence – that when he spoke, everyone paid attention!)

Power-as-capacity is inclusive and engaging, drawing people into communities and collaborations. Whether in individuals or groups, power-as-capacity is based on self-understanding but, at the same time, a commitment to the common good. This is the type of power that allows people to accomplish things together.

In any case, one of our most needed tasks over the next 20 to 50 years will be to redefine leadership so that it contributes to building a new and better social order and helps individuals find meaning and significance in their lives . . . your lives.

We've already discussed several shifts that our new definition of leadership permits. Among these, we highlighted the move from transactions to relationships, an emphasis on purpose and direction, and a shift from the exclusive use of soft skills to an increasing use of what we called the "squishy skills." But, as we discussed these changes, I mentioned there was still one other element that I wanted to add. I thought it was necessary to lay considerable groundwork for this addition to our approach to leadership. That being done, let's see how we might further add to our new formulation of leadership.

Amending Our Definition

Earlier I mentioned that the term "leadership" has been used, albeit rarely, to express the capabilities and character of someone who might lead. This counterpoint to the contemporary definition of leadership as being based on power and position strikes me as being closely allied with power-as-capacity. This interpretation of leadership, which deserves far greater currency, embraces both the capabilities and character of the potential leader. (Note – In what I'm about to write I recognize the male-centric nature of terms such as "craftsmanship" or "sportsmanship." While I like what these terms say about capability and character, I don't buy into the gender limitations they imply.)

In terms of capabilities, this understanding of leadership is similar to "craftsmanship" or "seamanship." It emphasizes the special skills needed to achieve excellence in a particular area. There is at least an implication that the skills are developed over a long period of time and perhaps with the aid of mentors and instructors. As a result, the craftsman has both the special understanding of the craft, an insight into the craft that others do not, and highly developed talents in the design and execution of the craft. In the same way, a leader brings a certain spirit of community to the work, a set of personal and group skills, and a special energy to the group or organization.

In terms of character, this alternative interpretation of leadership is more like "sportsmanship" or "companionship." It emphasizes the importance of honor and commitment. There is an understanding that the one who exhibits sportsmanship or companionship has either a highly tuned sense of responsibility or a moral commitment to another or to the job itself. As a result, the sportsman (or companion) is someone who doesn't merely "play by the rules," but has a special respect for the game or the relationship, which affects the way they act before, during, and after the immediate experience. For the leader, this understanding implies a sense of honor and respect, not the honor and respect others give to the leader, but the honor and respect the leader gives to the act of leadership. It's not the same as the phrase "respect for the office," since there is no office. But it is similar: it indicates respect for the work the leader does and the sense of responsibility that goes with leadership.

I think we could build a good case for restoring to the term "leadership" the same sense of capability and commitment that we have seen in these other examples (without the male-centric language.). Leadership, in that sense, would involve a high level of skill and a refined sense of moral responsibility, both developed over a long period of intellectual, emotional, and experiential growth. It would evoke a sense of finely tuned skill and a type of presence that we often long for but rarely see in our leaders today. Unfortunately, there is already so much confusion around the terms "leader" and "leadership" that adding this additional dimension would only confuse matters further. I would, however, urge that you give some thought to this idea, and perhaps together we can come up with a way of talking about leadership that always embraces not only skills, but honor and responsibility.

The Future of Leadership

To conclude this letter, let's see if we can catch a glimpse of the future of leadership. For that future to emerge, I think several things have to happen. But it's up to you and your generation to bring about meaningful change in leadership and organizations, and to do so in a way that is consistent with your values. This is my challenge to you.

First, you and other young and emerging leaders will have to end, or at least substantially decrease, our dependence on power as a driving force in getting things done. For thousands of years, what we have called "power-as-coercion" has moved groups and organizations and societies as they attempt to bring about change. Our reliance on power as a driving force has meant that we have been blind to other forces that energize people and cause them to act, forces such as caring, compassion, and love.

When you stop and think about it, it's easy to see how forces such as caring, compassion, and love are prime motivators in our lives, with love being surely as strong a motive as power. We can think of example after example where love overcomes hate or caring displaces power. We tend to use caring, compassion, and love to shape and motivate us in our private lives and employ power in our more public and work lives. In my view, there is no rational explanation for that, other than that we have been shaped and molded into creatures reflecting a historic dependence on power, and, some would say, exploitation. Kayla, this is the "hidden force" that you mentioned in one of your first letters. It's the force of our socialization into a power-oriented society.

Our society is so addicted to power that we strain to imagine alternative driving forces. While it may not be possible to fully eliminate power from our social diet, we can certainly cut down on our reliance on power-as-coercion in leadership.

Without question, changing that set of expectations will be very difficult and will take an extraordinary amount of time, decades at least. However, to the extent you can throw off the cultural chains that bind us to power as the default explanation for most of what we do, new possibilities will open to us. And the most dramatic and most attractive of those will be to default to love rather than power.

Second, as power-as-coercion recedes, power-as-capacity will likely advance. As it does, the opportunities for engaging with others in acts of shared interests, community interests, and, more generally, the public interest, will become both more obvious and more valued. Opening these possibilities will move people to act, propelled by a desire for autonomy based in a strong sense of community.

Third, your generation will need to create mechanisms through which people can collaborate for the common good. To allow greater individual choice does not mean chaos or anarchy. Instead, it means finding alternative ways of bringing people together to get things done. As just one example, imagine a technologically based system that would allow members of an organization to "bid" on heading those projects they found most valuable and most interesting.

Imagine also that a similar process was used to identify members of the team that would work on this project. Here, you would expect people to come to this project based on their interest in it, the contribution they felt they could make to it, and whether or not they felt it was meaningful and important. You would expect a better outcome than if members were "assigned" to the team. (How many times have you heard someone start a meeting by saying, "I don't know why they chose me"?).

This recalls our preference for relationships rather than transactions. Relationships are not simply based on a rational calculus of win – lose exchanges, but they incorporate intuition, emotions, and feelings. I sense that more and more people now recognize that work and its rewards are not the only drivers of satisfaction or happiness in one's life. As with any of the shifts we are talking about, this one has already exhibited ebb and flow, moving forward, then receding, accelerating in one part of the world or one sector of work, then pulling back there as others take hold.

What is important about this shift, especially when accompanied by movement away from power-as-coercion, is that it opens the possibility for much more effective human communications. We have already noted the distorting influence of power-as-coercion on communication in today's organizations and suggested communications will be enhanced in situations devoid of such relationships. Similarly, when human relationships replace transactions, communications will also improve.

Genuine human relationships require empathetic and supportive communications that contribute to building community as well as interpersonal understanding. Consequently, emphasizing power-as-capacity contributes to more effective communications and vice versa.

How Would It Feel?

We have a habit of talking about organizations in terms of spatial representations, such as the organization chart, and that leads us to ask what would an alternative "look like." We are so accustomed to organizational structures of power (power-as-coercion), that it's very hard for us to answer that question by visualizing what any alternative would look like. But maybe what an alternative "looks like" is not the question. Maybe we might ask instead what the alternative would "feel" like. What would be the sense of its movement through time? What would be the emotional conduit through which it flows?

The spatial representation of organizations (what it looks like) leads inevitably to the use of rational and objective criteria for its evaluation. However, the human experience of leadership in organizations (what it feels like) brings emotion, intuition, empathy, and love into the evaluation. This returns us to the leader within, for our commitments and our character are shaped less by the head, than by the heart.

I would venture to guess that a new leadership such as we've been describing would open more opportunities for mutual exchange and free-flowing interactions. Specifically, it would encourage communications unimpeded by the influence of power and coercion. It would feel less rigid, less stressful, and less confining.

All of these changes obviously decrease the need for management and increase the need for leadership, not the old leadership that equates with executive management, but a new leadership based on human relationships rather than transactions, one emphasizing a sense of meaning, purpose, and direction, and one recognizing skills such as empathetic communications and others. (Let's say "squishy" one more time). Moreover, it would feature pure rather than distorted communications, the twin values of character and community, and engagement rather than power. It would return leadership to its proper balance point between aspiration and inspiration.

This is the type of leadership described in my long academic definition of leadership and in my one-word definition of leadership as "energizing." It is the type of leadership that embraces both capability and commitment. It is the leadership of Mari on the playground and of Cooper at the university. And, Kayla and Mike, I hope it will be your leadership as well.

Yours,

Bob

26
LETTER FROM BOB
April 12

Dear Kayla and Mike,

Kayla, thanks for reminding me that I promised to address some of the special concerns of young and aspiring women as they move along in their leadership journey. There is no question that there are serious problems reflecting systemic bias and discrimination against women (and minorities) in our society. Many of these are policy issues, such as pay equity, parental leave, and bias in the hiring process, and should be addressed in the policy arena. I will try, on the other hand, to highlight more personal matters related to leadership itself, that is, concerns that affect women's efforts to lead.

I recognize that this topic poses a dilemma for me. If I were to avoid these issues, I might be accused of dismissing a set of leadership issues important to young women. On the other hand, if I address them, a question might be raised about my commenting on these issues without the experience of being a woman.

I understand both points of view, but I'm going to proceed anyway, hoping to represent what I hear both younger and older women (and men) saying about these concerns and how they might be addressed. For me to shy away from this aspect of leadership would be playing "intellectual dodgeball." And I promised at the outset not to do that.

There's another assumption that I make in this discussion – that this topic is of importance to both men and women. That is, while women must take the lead in articulating these issues, men must play a more substantial role in addressing gender bias, beginning by examining their own prejudices, and then helping construct a more balanced playing field for the development of more effective leaders, both men and women. So, Mike, this letter is not just to Kayla but to you (and me) too.

Leadership Issues Facing Women

By most accounts, the old view that men are more effective leaders than women is slowly fading away – though it certainly has not disappeared. A more modern iteration of this viewpoint, however, is getting increasing "play." It has to do with the leadership skills we discussed earlier. You will remember that I drew a contrast between two kinds of skills, the more familiar soft or transactional skills, including such things as communications, motivation, delegation, and conflict resolution, and the squishy or relationship skills, including such skills as empathy, tolerance, caring, and compassion, only now being fully recognized for their importance to leadership.

There are many who would say that transactional skills are more associated with the masculine, while relational skills are more associated with the feminine. (We might call this "the myth of gendered leadership.") By that, they imply that men have a "built-in" advantage in terms of the more rational and objective transactional skills, the skills of exchange, while women have an advantage in terms of the more empathetic and intuitive relationship skills. That's certainly not to say that women don't have or cannot develop transactional skills, nor that men don't have or cannot develop relational skills. Indeed, I would think that, wherever you stand in terms of your skills, you can improve your capacities.

But, in any case, there seems to be a widespread assumption today that leadership skills are, at least to some extent, distributed along gender lines. As scholars and practitioners have explored the different approaches men and women presumably bring to leadership, many have asked whether women moving into high-level positions in public, private, or nonprofit organizations would simply fall into the kinds of behaviors that men have traditionally exhibited as part of the old model of leadership – or whether they would bring with them a set of skills and perspectives that would help move our thinking about leadership in organizations, and elsewhere, in a new direction. As an increasing number of women entered the workplace, many managers speculated that these women would demonstrate more humanistic and relationship-oriented values, and would move others to increasingly adopt these values.

I helped write an article in the mid-1980s that asked this exact question, and we essentially concluded that it was too early to tell. I'm afraid that if we asked the same question today, decades later, we might give the same answer, though I suspect that there are many more forces moving in the direction of a more humanistic leadership today than before.

Over the last few decades, many male managers began to understand (if not to practice) what was to them a new approach, one that required sharpening their intuitive, empathetic, and relational skills. They learned listening skills, the advantages of consultation and shared power, and they engaged in various behavioral techniques, such as organizational development interventions.

The values promoted in these exercises were much like the core values reported to be held by the new wave of women coming into the workplace. These women sought a sense of connection, inclusion, and participation, and they often demonstrated the relational skills that were important to their new leadership.

These emerging women leaders were, of course, pressured in the other direction – to become more directive and "hardnosed" in their management styles, and many adopted the traditional top-down hierarchical mode of leadership and management that was familiar to men in the organization.

But the roots of sexism run deep, and many men exhibited outright resistance to women becoming managers or leaders. And some men came to work for women who were just as tough as these men perceived themselves to be, and their response was to use unfair and demeaning characterizations of their new bosses (and that's not the only b-word they used). It was one thing for them to work for a tough male boss, but quite another for them to work for a tough female boss.

There were other confusions as well. For example, someone (male or female) who perceives women as strong in relational skills but limited in transactional skills might see women as not standing up for themselves and their organizations, "folding" too easily in the face of strong opposition.

In turn, many women, hearing this critique, might wonder whether it was accurate and begin to either doubt their own strength and capabilities, or to succumb to the pressures to "be strong." But this can backfire. The female leader might be portrayed as being too strong "for a woman."

The psychological acceptance of this interpretation might lead young and emerging women leaders to say something like, "One thing I need to work on is my ability to stand up to difficult people and to deal with conflict." Indeed, this is not only something that I hear from young and aspiring women but, of course, is a part of what I heard from you, Kayla. But let's be sure not to blame the victim and imply that these young women can fix things if they just try.

What about the other side of this issue? I rarely hear aspiring male leaders say that they are too strong, strength still presumably being a masculine attribute. On the other hand, I occasionally hear men who have more successfully adopted a more open leadership style being described, often behind their backs, as too weak. The myth of gendered leadership has lots of victims along the way.

A related issue has to do with the willingness and capacity of young women to negotiate hard issues, especially issues that have to do with their own advancement. For example, many observers of life in large organizations have suggested that women have a harder time negotiating promotions and pay raises than men.

And indeed, in the experience of many women with whom I have talked, the prelude to negotiations – to ask – is often even more difficult than the negotiation itself. Historically, many women were socialized not to ask for what they wanted. There are likely psychological traces of that history remaining.

Similarly, the conventional wisdom still holds that women are more prone to the "imposter syndrome" than men (though men are not immune). That syndrome describes a situation in which individuals feel that they are in over their heads, and worry that someone will reveal them as the imposters they think they are.

A variation of this idea is that men are willing to accept a new job, knowing they don't possess all the skills needed for the job but expecting they can grow into it. Women, it is said, wait until they are fully prepared to do the job before they move into that job. I heard a recent speech by a well-placed state government official in which she reported on a hiring process in which four out of the five women candidates, upon hearing details of the job, said they needed more training before taking the job, while all five of the men said, "I'm ready."

Kayla, do you remember saying that you thought the men with whom you worked appreciated what you do, but failed to acknowledge or respect it? That again is a theme I hear from many young women. Too often they find themselves in the position of backing up or covering for the men in the organization. And while they know that the organization benefits from what they do, they also know that the men they work with, or for, will receive the credit.

Similarly, many young women report having said something in a meeting only to have their comment completely ignored, and then later, a man says exactly the same thing and gets credit for a brilliant idea. Of course, once more, men can be ignored as well, but this seems to happen more often to women.

Power relationships between men and women are not only difficult but deeply embedded in our personal and collective consciousness. You will remember that even some of the most distinguished ancient philosophers defended the rule of men over women. Over the centuries, women found few opportunities to lead outside the household, and even there, they were supposed to be subservient to men. We should remember that the movement for women's rights, even in so-called "advanced" countries, has a comparatively short history.

That is not to say that all or even most women have not fought back. Over the course of history, there have been many women who broke through what was then an "iron ceiling" (even more prohibitive than glass), and assumed significant leadership roles. At the same time, many other women sought ways to break free of male domination, using strategies ranging from the subtle to the dramatic. Coercion always triggers resistance, subtle or manifest – as it should.

More on Women and Power

Discussions of power have been important in the women's movement throughout its history but are becoming more frequent. One Jungian analyst contrasts what she calls the "masculine principle" with the "feminine principle," principles which can be exhibited by either men or women. (Another expression of the myth of gendered leadership.) The former principle is much like what we've called "traditional power," or "power-as-coercion." The latter principle, much like our notion of power-as-capacity, is focused on presence, relatedness, and connectedness.

Although probably overstating the case, some argue that Hillary Clinton is a woman who has become comfortable in the world of traditional power, and plays that game skillfully and hard. Michelle Obama, on the other hand, they say, exhibits presence and authenticity.

This question is equally interesting when you apply the same categories in describing their husbands. Certainly, Bill Clinton is perceived as comfortable in the world of power politics but has also blatantly played out some of the most outrageous male archetypes – for example, the "womanizer." On the other hand, Barack Obama, when he appeared to exhibit presence and authenticity, was sometimes accused of being weak and professorial.

We should also note the power differences involved in the issue of "standing." Recall that a potential leader's standing can be based on many things, such as previous reputation and experience, an introduction and show of support by respected others, or the prospective leader's own presence or, in our terms, energy. Some have said that visibility is a special concern for women – visibility, in this case, meaning being seen, being recognized as fully present in your own eyes and the eyes of others.

Many women grew up in families in which they weren't "seen," a condition also found in even today's workplace. Obviously, calls for women to "lean in" suggest one way of increasing female visibility and standing, but also comes very close again to blaming the victim, by implying that, by behaving differently, women can fix their own problems. In contrast, I would say that these issues reflect differences in power, and won't be resolved until power-as-coercion is eliminated as the basis for leadership and organization. (Notice I said "eliminated," not redistributed. The latter would merely redistribute the problem.)

Going back to the issue of standing: standing is enhanced by knowing those higher in the organization or in similar organizations and by having them as mentors, something that has historically been easier for men. The "good ol' boys' network" has been an advantage for men seeking standing with respect to leadership, but it is slowly, very slowly breaking down.

On the other hand, if there has indeed been a similar "women's network," there are signs that it too is breaking down. An interesting debate occurred in the 2016 presidential primary, a debate between older feminists and younger women voters. Madeleine Albright, for example, reminded potential voters that there is "a special place in hell" for those women who don't support other women, like then candidate Hillary Clinton. Young women commentators on CNN reacted immediately to that comment by saying that both men and women should vote for the person they think is best equipped to be president, regardless of gender.

Networks of men and women together have yet to be clearly established, in part because they raise difficult questions of their own. Obviously, such networks involve men and women socializing with members of the opposite sex, including lunches, dinners, and private meetings.

In either case, these occasions might be viewed – sometimes correctly, sometimes incorrectly – as opening the door to romantic and/or sexual relationships, potentially damaging both at work and at home (even assuming such relationships are fully consensual). Establishing the ground rules for men and women working together will be difficult for those involved, as well as difficult for their partners and families. (It can get a little strange. A female police officer commented: "I remember as a patrol deputy I had to tell my partner to stop opening the radio car door for me because we weren't on a date! He was just trying to be nice – but work is work!")

While men and women in the workplace have experienced some of the awkwardness and difficulties mentioned above, a typical discussion today involves nonconsensual relationships – sexual misconduct, sexual harassment, and sexual violence. Again, there is no question that these issues are based in the power differential between men and women in the workplace. They also reflect the withering of moral consciousness that, in many cases, accompanies increased power. Men who have engaged in misconduct, harassment, and violence toward women know that they are violating social norms, if not violating the law. Yet many continue to engage in the most distasteful and abusive practices, assuming that their power and position will conceal their acts from public notice. Once again, power masks moral transgressions, both from the public and even from the perpetrator himself.

But let's go back to the stages of establishing leadership. Having achieved standing, there are some ways women may have an advantage in the ensuing engagements with the group (assuming for a moment the widespread gendered view of leadership.) The advanced communication skills, especially the skills in empathetic communication attributed to women, as well as their consequent ability to create genuine human relationships (as opposed to transactions or exchanges) should be advantageous in the interactions between the potential leader and the group.

It's getting late. I'll follow up with this tomorrow.

Yours,

Bob

27
LETTER FROM BOB
April 14

Dear Kayla and Mike,

As you know, I wanted to discuss women in leadership because you raised the issue and because it's important to you and other aspiring young women (and men). But I'd be remiss if I didn't also acknowledge the roadblocks faced by people of color as they seek to lead.

Again, I must start with a disclaimer – I'm not black, nor brown. So, what I'm about to say is not based on my own experience but on research by minority scholars and on my conversations with young and aspiring minority leaders.

We can start with the fact that African-Americans and Latinos must navigate many of the same land mines that we've just discussed facing aspiring women leaders. They may find that their ideas and recommendations at meetings or conferences are more easily dismissed than those of their white colleagues. They may find that they have difficulty negotiating for pay and advancement, both because the evaluation process is often stacked against them, and because they must be careful that their arguments are not perceived as overly aggressive (fulfilling a negative stereotype). They may find themselves shunted into support roles or staff roles rather than steered toward mainstream leadership. And they may be told that in order to advance they need to have more leadership experience, yet they are not offered "stretch" assignments that would provide that experience.

But on top of these issues that are faced by other marginalized groups, there are some circumstances that affect racial minorities more than other groups – and here I'll focus mostly, but not exclusively, on African-Americans.

Our society is still marred by racism at all levels. Sometimes the way that racism is displayed is visible, as in attempts to suppress the voting rights of African-Americans. Sometimes it is subtle, as in what are called "microaggressions": "stunning, automatic acts of disregard that stem from unconscious attitudes of white superiority. . . ." These are the almost hidden slights that black folks encounter every day – the abrupt silence that occurs when they walk in on certain conversations, the assumption that each individual black person speaks for all black folks, or when someone says, "You're not like those other (black) people." While each individual act of aggression is "micro," the cumulative effect can be psychologically damaging to the individual and can restrict his or her progression toward leadership.

I also find the ideas of identity and self-concept helpful in thinking through the concerns of young and aspiring black leaders. Some scholars have argued that blacks tend to place race as the first component of their identity. That is, they self-identify first as blacks, and after that as parents, managers, teachers, or whatever they choose. Because race is such a large part of what black people experience, they tend to see things primarily through the lens of race.

Whites, so the argument goes, are less likely to put their racial identity first. As they define themselves, they are, say, first parents, second professionals, etc. – with being white coming somewhere later. For this reason, they rarely use the lens of race. It is a less salient part of their experience. But it may blind them (us) to the racial underpinnings of an otherwise innocuous exchange.

Given the different bases for their identity, those of different races will see things quite differently. A dispute over a project assignment may be seen by a black manager, looking through the primary lens of race, as a racial issue, while a white manager, looking through their primary lens as a businessperson, might see the dispute as simply reflecting a question of delegation. The white manager may not even recognize that there's a difference in interpretation, and proceed without acknowledging the racism inherent in the decision.

Even those whites who proclaim their support for blacks in the organization are not likely to fully understand the differences in demographics, experiences, and viewpoints between the races. They may think and they may say that they are "colorblind." They may say that they have "black friends" or they enjoy "black music." And, as individuals, they may indeed support their black colleagues. But that doesn't mean that there is not racism at play in their relationships, particularly those at work.

High-ranking white executives may talk a good game of diversity but fail to realize that many young black Americans don't even have the experience of knowing where to look for the path for leadership. They may not understand the value of a mentor or the opportunity that might be provided by an internship. The vast human potential that is wasted in this way is tragic, both for the individuals and for the society.

Certainly, the stereotypical images of different groups can often be subtly or even not so subtly played out in the workplace. A black female, for example, needs to be especially careful not to evoke the image of the "angry black woman." Her black male colleague may have to avoid being seen as "menacing," on the one hand, or "comical," on the other.

My friend Reuben shared an example from his recent campaign for political office. "You go door to door, introducing yourself to voters one by one. Every politician does it. But, when I was out door knocking, I had to always consider how these folks I was about to meet might respond to a strange black man standing in their doorway. So, I had to be very careful not to go in the evening, for fear that it could get dark outside. I had to be careful about how I dressed, when it was chilly, as people perceive a black man in a heavy winter coat and a hoody differently than they would a white man wearing the same clothes."

These and other damaging stereotypes are pervasive. For example, an award for the successful completion of a major project by a black employee may be considered the result of "affirmative action" or just plain luck. Meanwhile, a black employee's unsuccessful project is likely to draw more criticism than a white worker would receive – or a weak report might be dismissed as just what we would expect. Not surprisingly, black members of a group or organization feel they must work twice as hard as their white counterparts in order to get ahead. (Indeed, that's become a part of the black culture. A young African-American told me that at age 6 his father had a conversation with him, pointing out that in school he would have to perform twice as well as the white boy in the next chair.)

Even if young black people achieve a foothold on the path toward leadership, there are still limitations they must face, given the dominance of the white culture. Emerging black leaders experience subtle pressures to adopt patterns and practices that meet the standards of the white organization. But, at the same time, they are being pressured by their home communities to remain true to their black culture.

It's a delicate balance, one that aspiring black leaders must navigate every day. They must appear "focused at the office but not too aggressive; hungry but not threatening; well-dressed but not showy; talented but not too damn talented." Playing this game daily can be frustrating, even debilitating.

At the same time, these pioneers are pressed to remain true to the black community. The first few to join are likely to feel an obligation to mentor and support those who are coming after them. They may also be called upon to serve on every committee or project team that is formed, because, in addition to their talent, the company wants to look good in terms of diversity. The black manager may agree to join the group, not necessarily because it serves the company's interest, but because serving on such committees may position them to help others from their community. But these activities take time away from their doing the job they were hired for, much less allowing them to compile a record of leadership experience and advancement.

All of this becomes even more complicated when you throw the categories of gender and race together. Each group must contend with its own set of stereotypes. For example, Latinas who behave assertively are often seen as angry or emotional, even when they report they weren't at all angry but just were not deferential. Nearly 60 percent of Latinas report a backlash against expressing anger as well as being given a disproportionate amount of office housework – even by other women. Incidentally, the widespread advice for women to "lean in" may be problematic for black women and Latinas, for whom leaning in may be a taken as aggression.

My friend Jasmin suggests that the warm and supportive behaviors that would lead to a Latina being described as a "good woman" in the household are at odds with those characteristics that would have them described as a "good leader" in the corporate or governmental world. For a Latina to be both a good woman and a good leader requires almost a splitting of her personality, or at least a difficult balancing of supportiveness and independence. And, as Jasmin points out, a Latina should avoid anything that brings up the stereotype of either the hotel maid in uniform, even to the point of not helping clean up the room after a meeting. This presents an obvious dilemma, since much of the current literature on leadership recommends that the leader occasionally help out with even the most mundane tasks.

Isn't It About Power? Of Course It Is

Some of the roadblocks we have discussed facing women and minorities are things that men experience as well – for example, not being heard in a meeting. But there is an important difference. Women and minorities have been subject to sexism and racism for centuries – and that's a history, a reality, that can't be dismissed. It still permeates the relationship between the sexes and races in all kinds of ways. We can't escape the fact that discrimination, historically and still today, is rooted in power and its abuse.

In my view, power cannot operate without bias. It inherently says some are to direct and others are to be directed. From there, it's a short step to saying one group is superior, better than the other. And from there it's only another short step to saying that's the way it should be, that those who hold power are morally superior as well. They have a right to power.

For women and minorities, power differences are not just "in their heads." They are real and must be dealt with realistically. Women and minorities must be mindful of differences in power and the power of perceptions. They are in the awkward position of dealing with perceptions held by others, with self-perceptions influenced by others, and with the reality of power differences – all at the same time. What a difficult complex of ideas and images to navigate!

Going Forward

I suppose the key point is that diversity and inclusiveness are hallmarks of a free and open caring society, one that pays attention to the needs of all, both inside and outside the organization. It seems to me that this is an important point with respect to the future of leadership. Already, major corporations and government agencies are recognizing that their constituencies are becoming more and more diverse and that they must respond to that circumstance by becoming more diverse themselves. Representation of all segments of society in the organization means that it can respond to the collective needs of the community with greater effectiveness. Lacking such representation, organizations become dependent on power relationships, internally and externally. There is the power that those higher in the organization have over their employees and the power that organizations use to shape the consumer demand for their products.

Our markets are not free, in the sense of giving individuals unfettered choice. Corporations spend millions of dollars to create a market for their products. "Consumer behavior" is very much like traditional "organizational behavior," in that both are based on exchanges and transactions, and the issue simply becomes, how can you manipulate those exchanges to the greatest benefit of the organization? The result is that communications between the consumer and the producer are distorted and the lack of trust builds.

When we talk about diversity and inclusion, on the other hand, we are clearly talking about building power-as-capacity. Having more women and minorities involved in organizations expands the group's sensitivity to the needs and interests of many more of its constituents. Just as physical therapists talk about expanding the range of motion for an individual, greater diversity and inclusion can expand the range of connections for the organization.

What does this say about leadership? I think it becomes obvious that the leader or potential leader needs to be tuned into the concerns of women and minorities as well as white males. To the extent that the employees of any organization feel that their needs are not being met by the group, they will correspondingly limit or even withdraw their contributions. Remember that in order to lead you must engage and engage deeply. By that I mean that you must approach the ongoing dialogue not simply from the standpoint of your own frame of reference, but from the frame of reference of others who are different from you. How can you do that?

Well, at a minimum it requires a great deal of energy and engagement. Conversations with those who are unlike you, whether in terms of race, gender, economic background, psychological type, policy solutions – or any other difference – can be highly informative, but only if you listen carefully. That is why my first three recommendations for managers are to listen, listen, listen. For leaders, listening is even more important.

Our work culture and the larger culture in which it resides have both been changing rapidly over the past few decades and it is incumbent on those who would lead to be sensitive to those cultural changes. There is no reason to think that the period of change is over. In fact, there's every reason to think that it is just beginning – and that it will continue.

As it does, potential leaders, both men and women, and people of color, must avoid getting caught up in the more visible but, in the long term, more trivial questions such as "Are men or women better leaders?" As we move through periods of transition, both men and women of all races and ethnicities will face leadership challenges brought about, not by disagreements between gender or race, but by clashes of cultures and perceptions, political and economic interests, and global forces seemingly beyond anyone's power to understand (much less control). Over time, meaning decades, even centuries, gender and racial differences will be less important than developing leaders who have the skills, strategies, and spirit to take on these important challenges.

I have been suggesting that organizations will move toward more genuine relationships, but for the present, people largely communicate based on transactions. This means, Kayla and Mike, that both of you must develop those relationship capabilities that will be increasingly valuable, but that you will, for some time, operate in a system that values the opposite. In a sense, you may be on the cutting edge. But being on the cutting edge exposes you to nicks and scratches, including accusations of not being able to operate in the old world of transactions, especially in the world of hard-nosed negotiations.

I would encourage you to continue to develop your own relationship skills and those of others around you. Yet be aware of the stage of change that you are in, likely an early one, and learn to be comfortable in transactions as well as relationships.

Finally, be aware that you can't overgeneralize (as I probably have been). Not all women and certainly not all black folks would agree with much of what I've said here. Their individual experiences have differed in substantial ways. Similarly, not all women practice empathetic communications, and not all men avoid them. There are plenty of men (like Mike) who are learning skills such as empathetic communications and engaging in building relationships. And these men cannot only learn from you, Kayla, but they can and will be supportive of you in your leadership.

Indeed, you two provide a good illustration of a woman and a man who are allies in a quest for a new leadership. Together you and your contemporaries can make a dramatic difference in the practice of leadership today and tomorrow. And changing leadership in the way we have been describing will also promote shifts in freedom and autonomy in other realms such as gender and race, just as change in those areas promotes greater freedom and autonomy in our groups and organizations.

Yours,

Bob

28
LETTER FROM KAYLA
May 1

Bob

I really appreciate your addressing some of the concerns many young women have coming into the workplace these days. And I liked that you put this letter next to the others dealing with power and control, because I think that's what discrimination is all about. Women in our company and probably many others face a curious mix of responses from our male colleagues, responses ranging from easy acceptance to outright hostility. I think we are going in the right direction, but it takes so long to change patterns of discrimination. We still face various personal slights and prejudices, though many seem to have slipped beneath the surface, only to come out in times of stress or uncertainty. That's when the guys really want to push us aside and take over!

In some ways, the characterization of women focusing on relationships rather than transactions, searching for meaning and opportunities for personal development in our jobs (and being willing to move on if they're not there), being attentive to issues of work – life balance and, more generally, flexibility in the workplace, are the same as the more positive interpretations of the attitudes of millennials. More important, these seem to be the qualities that you are describing in the new leadership.

So, when you ask where the momentum for change might come from, I would say that young women constitute a wellspring of support for the changes you are talking about, though there seem to be a lot of my peers who could care less about these issues. We need to mobilize many of them in order to bring about change. However, neither millennials as a group nor women as a group speak a single language. For that reason, it's important to recognize that different streams of thought may appear, and then disappear in any effort to change society.

I guess the question for me, both personally and as an aspiring woman leader, is this – do I have enough courage to take on the challenge of changing leadership in my world? While I may be hesitant in asserting myself in other ways, there's something about this particular issue that makes me want to act. I commented earlier about my being a "fighter," which indeed I am when I'm really challenged. Maybe I feel the challenge most strongly with respect to these issues.

As you said, the change we are describing may be slow in coming about. In fact, I think you said it might take 100 or more years, maybe 200. I'd like to see some changes come about more quickly than that, at least in my lifetime, but if I can join with other young women in starting the process, that would be an important first step. This would be meaningful work for me and would answer the question of why we should get involved in leading others (a question we haven't talked much about yet).

But however this shakes out in the long run, I'm ready to take this on. I'm sure that, along the way, we will continue to face both structural discrimination and sexism at the personal level. But the next time a clearly sexist idiot like Howard Clark asks me to get him some coffee before a meeting, I may get the coffee, but I will ask to talk with him later about our respective roles in the organization. I'll be nice. But, still, I bet that in my gut, I will picture spilling my hot coffee all over his ridiculous plaid shirt and bow tie!

Kayla

P.S. Okay, I overstated that. This coffee thing is an annoyance, but those areas of discrimination we just talked about are much more important. Thanks again for addressing them!

29
LETTER FROM MIKE
May 5

Bob

I too want to thank you for addressing the concerns facing young men and young women and majorities and minorities today as we seek to understand our changing roles and responsibilities vis-à-vis one another. I suppose the relationship between men and women has been challenging at best from the beginning of time. Some parts of that relationship are elemental, inherent parts of our being human. I'm thinking of the mixture of love, sex, commitment, the dynamics of family life, growing up, aging together, dying alone, and grieving for one another. With all those ingredients, how could the resulting stew be more complex? How could it not be served in so many ways – from hot to cold, from sweet to sour? How could it not be received in so many ways – from sustenance to revelry, from small bites to sheer gluttony? And how could it not cause such different reactions – from joy to sorrow, from pleasure to excess, from indulgence to regret?

(I guess my father's poetic language and biblical imagery kicked in there. I can still hear his voice ringing from the pulpit, saying "I am the Bread of Life. Whoever comes to me shall not hunger, and whoever trusts in me shall never thirst.")

I remember someone saying that all interactions in organizations carry with them sexual overtones. But, as you pointed out, when those sexual overtones are mixed with power, all bets are off.

Certainly, men of previous generations have behaved badly, often very badly, towards women generally, and, more specifically, in the workplace. All the recent accusations and revelations of sexual misconduct and sexual harassment on the part of men in positions of power demonstrate, as you point out, the immorality of power.

What about my male contemporaries? Most have come to accept, albeit for some grudgingly, the notion of equal pay and promotions, etc. – the policy issues you mentioned earlier. But few have signed on to combat the psychological residue of the exploitation of women that you presented. There are relatively few of my male contemporaries who would call themselves "feminists," and even fewer whose women colleagues would describe in that way. But there are plenty who would support a new leadership that promoted equality among men and women, as well as other groups. Maybe this is a chink in the armor of coercive power.

Your discussion of roadblocks facing people of color was interesting to me in a couple of ways. First, you pointed out that many of the same issues faced by women in organizations are faced by minorities. Second, you wrote that there were some special circumstances faced by minorities seeking to lead. You mentioned microaggressions and stereotyping as problems, then analyzed those problems by looking at the identity issue. That there are these differences makes sense to me.

Your discussion of women and leadership pointed out that there may be a masculine and feminine interpretation of leadership. Do you think there's a white interpretation of leadership and a black interpretation.? Certainly, from what I understand, black society is more collectivist or communal than white. If so, you would expect that black leadership would be more engaging, more transparent, and more sensitive to the needs of members of the group. But this is just speculation at this point. I don't know of any research that would support this, do you?

Of course, as you pointed out, many black leaders found it necessary to adapt to white cultural standards in order to advance. The feminine leadership may challenge masculine leadership. But my guess is that even if there is a black leadership, it would have great difficulty challenging the existing white leadership – except that it adds support to the view you've talking about here, a view which is also compatible with the feminine leadership model. There does seem to be a cluster of ideas coming together.

In any case, I agree with you that this is all about power. And it's not just a misuse of power. These concerns are inherent in situations in which one person has power over another. The power advantage of some leads to their taking advantage of others. And, again, as you say, there are power holders who believe they are somehow superior to others and therefore morally justified in their mistreatment.

I sometimes think about how our "enlightened" society thinks about the history of slavery. After 2,000 years we took slavery to be an important diminution of individual rights. As you can talk about changes in leadership in organizations, I've come to wonder whether in 200 or 500 or a thousand years people will look back on the way that we structured our leadership and organizations today as similarly barbaric. I wouldn't be surprised. But I doubt that any of us will be around to celebrate that.

One last thing. It has been apparent that the most visible cases of sexual misconduct revealed over the last couple of years have involved extraordinarily powerful men (mostly white men). But their behavior is merely the most conspicuous. The abuse of women in the workplace is carried out at all levels. This understanding has caused many men to carefully reflect on their own histories. Are they guilty themselves in some way? Did they inadvertently engage in distasteful rhetoric? Did they purposely or even accidentally touch someone in the wrong place? More to the point, did they ever engage in gender discrimination or sexual misconduct themselves? Did they fail to speak up when others acted badly?

These are important questions and deserve close scrutiny. In fact, many men would probably benefit from an even larger dose of self-reflection and self-critique around these issues of discrimination and exploitation. (Maybe we could develop a 12-step program through which men could address concerns like these, with respect to both gender and race.) But the bottom line for me is this – I recognize that remnants of sex discrimination and racial stereotypes still are a part of me – even though I consider myself pretty progressive on these issues. This is a fight to which I'd certainly lend my support, recognizing again, as we have before, that change must begin within.

Mike

30
LETTER FROM BOB
May 15

Dear Kayla and Mike,

We've been vacationing in Scandinavia, mostly Iceland, Norway, and Finland, and we are right now on a plane heading back to California. It's been a marvelous trip, and we found Norway especially beautiful – the fjords, the ferries, the mountains and waterfalls, and the color and excitement of the cities. I tried hard not to work during our time away, but I thought of you and our letters often.

Kayla, your most recent letter was eloquent in stating the challenges and opportunities you face as a young female leader. I know you have given serious consideration to the obstacles that you will face moving toward leadership. But even beyond that, your acceptance of these challenges and your willingness to take them on comes from a great deal of self-reflection on your part. And I think the level of psychological maturity you have gained will aid you considerably as you move along your journey.

I hope other young women find your words inspiring and also accept the challenge of creating a new leadership, as you have. Yes, I do think it will take a long time to achieve, but the sooner we get started, the better we will be. Thanks again.

And, Mike, I appreciate your providing such a compelling commentary on the role of young men in these struggles. And I really enjoyed your poetic excursion!

But for now, let me speak to one of the very first issues that both of you raised early on in our exchanges and one we have just come back to – the question of how you might bring about change.

I've waited until now to address this issue because I thought there were some other things that needed to come first. Specifically, I wanted to illustrate some of the problems the old models of leadership in organizations have spawned, and outline a few of the changes I would recommend in thinking about and practicing leadership. But now we need to turn to more clearly examine the personal experience of leadership, what it feels like. This will bring us back around to the leader within.

Upon reading these pages, you have said what many other young and emerging leaders say about my views: "I find your ideas attractive, but I just don't see how they can be put into practice. Even if I commit to this approach, how will I fare in the real world in which I live and work? Am I simply opening myself up to being run over by others? What can I do to make a difference?" These are important questions, and you are right in raising them. The old model is deeply ingrained in our individual and collective consciousness, and for us to even think about alternatives is difficult. We hear the words, we understand the words, we may even believe the words, but we can't imagine living the words.

Again, the old model is the model you were taught by your parents, by your teachers, by your employers, and by your friends. It is a model you have employed in dealing with other people at work, as well as in social groups and even in your family. It is a model that has been reinforced by stories from your childhood, games you played growing up, experiences you had in school, expectations of you as you entered the workplace, and through social and cultural definitions of "success."

As a result of these influences, you have very likely come to accept a particular set of ideas that I mentioned in an early letter: we find it natural to come together to get specific things done, to meet our goals; we structure our activities by dividing the work so that everyone knows what to do; we interact with others through exchanges or transactions; we are assigned work by someone in a position of power and authority; and we think that ethics consists of a group of rules that we should follow but that are often bent, especially by those with the most power.

These ideas are persuasive because they make sense logically, because we have seen them work time after time, and because they are deeply embedded in our culture, especially as it relates to work and organization. Such a powerful set of beliefs, we reason, must be right.

This is a thorny question, however. I just wrote that "we reason" that those beliefs must be right. And if you carefully think about them, you will likely agree that they make sense rationally. Inquire into their practical or their intellectual history and you will find a deep and enduring rationale for these ideas: over and over throughout history, people have reasoned that these beliefs would help groups get things done. More importantly, leaders and rulers themselves reasoned that these beliefs would help them achieve their goals, and have not only endorsed but often enforced them.

Likely, however, most people today don't reason through these beliefs. Nor do they ask whether these beliefs are still appropriate to today's and tomorrow's society. They simply accept them as a matter of custom, a part of the culture. Although these ideas were historically a practical solution to human problems, they have become a cultural belief system, a pattern of human understandings shared by many. They have then been passed down through the generations with some variations, but with the basics largely intact.

Against this backdrop of basic assumptions, our thinking about leadership in organizations has evolved. We have moved from the raw power, coercion, and violence that sustained early rulers, to the subtle political manipulation that Machiavelli championed, to the current wave of shared power. These are important shifts in our thinking, but not the kind of paradigmatic change that we now find necessary. (For example, if you are in the position to share power, you must have power to share. Coercion is still a possibility.) These changes represent points along the continuum moving from domination to autonomy, but all still remain securely embedded in the domination side of the equation. Though much has changed, much has stayed the same.

In the march toward autonomy, we still have a long way to go. The use of power-as-coercion is still present, though it may be subtler. Employee autonomy and involvement has widened, though, in a relative sense, only marginally. The traditional model is now so strong that we do things not because the boss uses or threatens force, but because we have come to expect that when the boss tells us what to do, we do it.

The strength of acculturation is so great that the use of power today need not be as obvious as in earlier times. But power is still part of our consciousness. The roots of rulership run deep within our collective memories, ready to burst forth when the pressure on executives causes them, often without even thinking about it, to go back to those roots.

But new circumstances and new attitudes cry out for a different model of leadership in organizations. In contrast to the old model of organization that boasts of consistency and dependability (qualities that were important in industrial times), the new model emphasizes the importance of speed and agility, autonomy and choice, creativity and adaptability. In contrast to the old model of leadership that depends on rational planning and hierarchical power, the new model centers on empathy, caring, compassion, and love. The change is not only underway, it is inevitable.

Where will change come from? It may surprise you, but I don't think it will come from the academy, which, in many ways, provides support for the existing model. Of course, it's no wonder that scholars take this position because, while few are members of the economic elite, many have valuable contacts within the upper ranks of corporate America and earn healthy consulting incomes based on those contacts (even beyond their secure university salaries) – and even those who don't benefit financially live in a society that values productivity, so they consequently orient their research to that end.

Scholars who study leadership, for example, write about ethical leadership or authentic leadership, but hardly in revolutionary terms. Indeed, university-based researchers tend to reinforce the status quo with respect to leadership in organizations. The central question, the one that is most frequently posed is this: what conditions and what leader/manager behaviors will lead to greater efficiency and productivity? For example, does "authentic" leadership result in greater productivity? This is simply scholarship in the service of power. Among college and university faculty, conformity to the existing norms is prevalent and critique is limited (and hidden in letters like these – shh!).

So where might a movement to drastically alter our understanding of leadership in organizations begin? Could a movement for change come from within organizations themselves? Certainly, it is not likely to come from the top, where power holders benefit from maintaining the current model. Indeed, that is where we would expect the most opposition.

There is, however, one exception. If autonomy is proven to increase productivity, those at the top are likely to immediately jump on board. But that leads to some interesting and ironic tensions. My view is that autonomy is likely to increase productivity as we move through the coming decades. But if someone at the top tries to jump on the autonomy wagon, they will be necessarily giving up power, at least power-as-coercion. That may be too much for them to do.

Nor is change likely to come from the bottom, for people at that level don't have the resources nor the time to fully engage in reconstituting the existing culture of leading in organizations. Contrary to Marx, I doubt if the workers of the world will unite around this issue.

I think change will come about in three ways. First, young and emerging leaders, mostly inhabiting the midrange of large organizations and located somewhat higher in smaller organizations, will embrace new models of leadership and implement those models in their organizations. Second, the encroachment of the work culture into the rest of our lives will be challenged and perhaps reversed. Third, based on these individual changes and cultural changes, more and more people from the top to the bottom of organizations will begin experimenting with new forms of leadership. Let's take a look at each of these three steps.

First, the starting place in moving past the old model is to recognize that it is indeed a social and cultural invention, not something built into the "natural order of things." Since it is a social and cultural construction, it can be altered and eventually replaced by a different set of ideas and practices. As I keep saying, I think the change will take decades, maybe even centuries. But I'm also confident that your beliefs and practices, those of today's young leaders, can make a substantial difference in pointing us in the right direction.

There certainly are rational arguments for your generation to shift from the old model to something else: the old model is neither economically nor ecologically sustainable; it fails to meet the minimum requirements of democratic responsibility; its conservative tendencies don't encourage much needed creativity and innovation; and globalization and information technology have created a world in which rigid organizational structures must give way to flexibility and agility.

But a rational justification for change is not sufficient, particularly at the level of your individual work and life. You can't return to work tomorrow armed with this information and persuade your boss, your peers, and your subordinates to dramatically change the way they operate. Neither are you likely to get far by asking your boss for permission to do things differently. (Again, the term "permission" is interesting itself in that it acknowledges the power of the person who is being asked to permit you to do something. Permission is just another shade of power-as-coercion.)

We often speak of change within the current model of leading and organizing as coming either from "the top down" or "the bottom up." Change from the top implies an exercise of power. Change can be brought about through persuasion and influence, but in most situations of broad-scale organizational change, the fact that "the boss is always the boss" makes all the difference.

Change from the bottom up gives the appearance of a more democratic approach to leadership in organizations, but in practice, power usually is key here as well. Change from the bottom up is often mandated from the top or permitted by those at the top. And we should also note that executives and managers often create what appear to be bottom-up approaches to gain support for decisions already made. This is simply manipulation.

If you are in a small, informal organization, you may be able to bring about some changes in the typical patterns of interaction in the group. But even those changes will be difficult to introduce. If, on the other hand, you are in a large and more formal organization, your chances of moving the entire organization will be slim. Your efforts will be met by objections of all sorts – most notably from those who will lose power if change comes about, but also from those who simply fear change and cling tightly to the existing way of doing things.

There will also be resistance, active resistance. Those who are astute in playing the game of power will use the resource that has always worked for them in the past, power itself, to counter your suggestions. But you can't allow yourself to be dragged into a power struggle – first, because you will inevitably lose (they are simply better at this game than you are), and second, because your adopting power-as-coercion as a way of leading is itself an admission that you don't believe in your own alternative model.

Of course, your success in changing leadership in organizations will depend in part on your position in the organization. I suspect that younger middle managers, especially if allied with lower participants, will not only have the capacity but an interest in changing the way leadership is viewed. Moreover, they will be the ones that have the experience of being on the receiving end of coercion. They will see much more clearly the evidence of mistakes made at the higher level. They see what happens where the "rubber hits the road."

Some scholars have argued that revolutions in science begin when the existing paradigm fails to explain anomalies. Similarly, students of organizational change suggest that change sometimes requires a crisis to get everyone's attention at the outset. Certainly, we are beginning to recognize anomalies in the old model of leadership generally and leadership in organizations specifically. It may be that the anomalies that we can describe currently in abstract terms will require a specific crisis to move people to action. And I think there's every reason to believe that such a crisis will soon occur. It may be social, it may be economic, it may be environmental. (Indeed, in the latter area, the crisis may already be here.)

In any case, when the crisis occurs, proponents of an alternative way of doing things must be prepared to bring forward their ideas and their arguments. What we're talking about is leading the process of reforming leadership. But be aware that the culture that sustains the old model of leadership in organizations is deeply embedded and is an inherently conservative force.

Second, conceiving of an alternative to the old model is difficult, as difficult as describing a second dimension to someone who lives in the first. (Do you know the classic book, *Flatland*?) But I think there is one way in which we can at least get a hint as to what the new model might "feel like" by examining the other side of the work/life dichotomy. The beliefs that underlie our lives outside of organizations present a dramatic contrast with those beliefs we described earlier as characterizing our lives in organizations.

In our lives outside organizations, we seek valued but often ambiguous purposes: much of our time is unstructured or free-form; we seek genuine human relationships, characterized by empathy, transparency, caring, compassion, and love; we are guided in what we do, not by being told to do it, but by our ideas and emotions; and there are few (if any) rules that fit all situations, so we exercise moral imagination.

There are also reasons to suggest that there may be a cultural shift beginning. In my book, *In the Shadow of Organization*, I argued that the "rules" of life in organizations have crept over into our lives outside organizations to the point that we engage in transactions with others rather than building genuine human relationships, and we coerce and manipulate others rather than being guided by an ethic of caring, compassion, and love. What I'm now suggesting is that our life outside organizations may provide a basis for reforming leadership in organizations – for example, that we now focus on building genuine human relationships, acting based on power-as-capacity, and being guided by a refined moral consciousness.

We might almost describe a cultural battle between life and work, one in which work has increasingly encroached on our lives outside work, but one in which there is every reason to believe that the direction of the battle is about to shift. There are significant cultural indicators signaling a heightened interest in autonomy, purpose, meaningfulness, and a commitment to service.

Again, cutting across these developments is the massive impact of technology, especially information technology. That impact is not just felt in the way we accomplish technical tasks, but in the social and cultural milieu as well. Modern information technology raises difficult questions with respect to privacy, intrusiveness, and control. But it also offers support for unrestricted social interaction, the widespread dispersion of information, greater personal, social, and organizational agility, and support for both synchronous and asynchronous collaboration. These latter developments consistently align with the demands for autonomy and the like mentioned previously. In turn, they support, both technically and culturally, the new model of leadership and organization we have described here.

In my view, while the technical and economic issues associated with Advanced Technology are difficult, sorting out the social, cultural, political, and ethical issues will be the most important questions defining life itself in the coming centuries. (Again, my dictation equipment automatically capitalized Advanced Technology, which now apparently ranks with the Church and the Corporation. OK, Church, Corporation, and Advanced Technology. Are they all from the same family? They seem to be to my computer!)

Third, going back to the question of how change can be brought about, I have discussed personal transformation and cultural transformation. What remains, I think, is organizational transformation, including experiments with new forms of leadership.

Following the model of scientific revolutions, the appearance of anomalies leads to the search for new practices, new ways of conducting scientific inquiry. These new patterns address the anomalies and begin to challenge the old paradigm. I think we are at that point with respect to leadership in organizations. As a society, we have identified anomalies in the current pattern, and we are beginning to experiment with alternative practices. Some of these alternatives are being suggested by scholars and public intellectuals. Others are springing up in the "real world" of business and government.

The terms used to describe these alternatives are many – shared leadership, servant leadership, authentic leadership, radical management, open organization, holocracy, Google-ocracy, and more. But what all these efforts have in common is that they are seeking a new way of leading, a new way based on greater individual autonomy, genuine human relationships, and an ethic of service and responsibility.

Most of these experiments to date are modest and, even so, many will fail, but eventually a congruent set of ideas and practices will form into an alternative model of leadership in organizations. Throughout these letters, I have tried to suggest what that alternative model would look like, but even more important, feel like. In doing so, I consider these letters my own experiment in constructing the future of organizational leadership.

You'll also remember Mari on the playground and Cooper at the university, both of whom were engaged in real-life experiments in leading others and both of whom were highly successful. The two remind us that leadership as energizing occurs throughout society, and that the lessons for future leadership may be as easily found on the playground as in the boardroom.

And this brings the question back to you. Someone must be the first or the second or the fiftieth or the thousandth to try something new. Wherever you are, at whatever level or occupation, you have the capacity, indeed the obligation, to do what you can to advance your ideas and practices to solve immediate problems and to create new opportunities. You must also define and model a new leadership that others can follow.

As you and others experiment, engage with colleagues, draw meaning from your experiences, and communicate a new narrative, you will contribute to what will be a dramatic change in the way we lead. The change starts with you. It must draw from the leader within, but its effect, whether a ripple, a wave, or a tsunami, will be felt around you and around the world.

Yours,

Bob

31

LETTER FROM BOB

May 20

Dear Kayla and Mike

Why would you want to lead? There are a number of reasons. You may be called to lead by desperate circumstances in which you not only know the group but have some special understanding of the crisis. Or you may be called to lead by a group who knows you, knows of your past record of leading in other times and other places, and pressures you to come forward. There are situations where it is simply hard to turn down a request for you to lead. But it must be your choice. Consider your capabilities as a leader, your experience and your preparation for leadership, and the question we often forget to ask – whether you want to lead.

There certainly are some negatives that we need to consider:

- The pressure and stress of leading are constant.
- The responsibility of leading can be a heavy burden.
- You put your life on the line daily – not necessarily physically, but psychologically.

First, acts of leading eat up huge amounts of personal energy: they can be strenuous and stressful. They require paying close attention for lengthy amounts of time without a break, and they require careful and measured responses. They are physically as well as mentally draining – remember Cooper's relentless scheduling of meetings with various groups.

Acts of leading also require creativity and innovation in sorting through the group's rapidly changing issues and concerns. This too is hard work. Creativity and innovation are not just about sudden flashes of insight. They require always being curious and inquisitive, being open to new and often baffling possibilities, and being persistent in the face of doubt and disapproval.

Of course, added to all of this is the fact that everyone around you (or at least it seems like everyone) has his or her own special issues, requests, or demands. The pressure on you as a leader to articulate the initial narrative in a certain way is great, but the pressure on you to bend to demands from the inside or outside over time may be even greater. Whether you bend or not and whether you bend at the right time or not will affect your continued standing in the organization and your continued capacity to lead.

There will be good days, and there will be bad days. And there will be really bad days. And the really bad days may become bad weeks and bad months and so on. The reasons why bad times occur are many, but what's worse is that you probably will never figure out why. Sometimes it will seem as if the universe is plotting against you – and maybe some smaller forces are. More likely, an unexpected confluence of events elsewhere in the organization, an imperfect storm, probably somewhere above, is coming together in such a way that you become the lightning rod, although you had little or nothing to do with the issue. (Of course, you have to figure out whether this is the case or whether you actually screwed up!)

Second, and obviously related, leading carries with it responsibility, a commitment to the group, the community, and the larger public. For the leader, traveling the high road means dismissing self-interest and taking the larger interest of the community into account. The leader must take responsibility, not only for his or her own actions, but for the actions of the group as well. Even with the best intentions (and I assume that you will act with the best intentions!), you can misread the situation or misread the group, setting out a purpose and direction that is ill-timed and destructive. And you will pay the price.

Third, in such circumstances, you put your future on the line every day. In smaller settings, such as on the playground or the sports field, failures of leadership may result in your being shunned or dismissed by others. But even the best leadership can be misinterpreted by opponents, as in the case of a girls' soccer coach who was called "despicable" for his mentioning "winning." But, in such cases, you will recover – or just move on

Freud argued that there is always a psychological tendency for members of the group to want to symbolically "kill" the leader. Such a tendency is amplified in situations where people perceive that the leader has pointed the group in the wrong direction, where the leader has "mis-led" the group. At a minimum, the leader will lose standing; at a maximum, much worse.

I've tried to be careful here to stick closely to concerns about acts of leading as opposed to acts of execution or management. While acts of leading, or rather misleading, are punishable by loss of standing, failures of management are punishable by demotions, organizational exile, firing, and so on. But for the leader, standing is everything.

Given these circumstances, drawn from my own experience and the experience of others, it's hard to imagine why anyone would want to lead! It's too easy to screw up, and the penalties are personal and severe. So why take on the burden?

Because there are some incredible positives:

- You can make a difference in the world by effecting needed change.
- You can touch individual people in ways that transform their lives.
- You can challenge yourself to reach your own best potential.

First, we have discussed the many problems facing our world today. There are obviously dozens of important issues that cry out for attention and remedy: disease, poverty, hunger, violent conflict, mental illness, and global terror, to name just a few. In a diversely populated, yet highly connected global society, these issues seem to be magnified in their severity. Yet whatever the appropriate level of concern, it is clear that no one individual or small group is likely to come up with a solution to these problems, and even if a solution were found, its implementation on a global scale would require the mobilization of hundreds, if not thousands or even hundreds of thousands of people.

Mobilization, in this case, implies both leadership and management – leadership to energize the group, the organization, or the society, and management to coordinate the actions of many different parties focusing on the solution. Think how rewarding it would be to lead an effort that would solve even one segment of the problems we face today

But don't let me overwhelm you with thoughts of solving planetary crises. There are plenty of things you can do at home to lead in making your community a better place to live. Just look around you. Make connections with neighbors, friends, and associates, engage them in discussions about how to improve community life, add your own creative insight, tell the story, and trigger action. The rewards may be few in financial terms, but in terms of the satisfaction of making your world a better place, they can't be beat.

Second, the rewards of leadership come not only from building a better future for your community or beyond, but at a more personal level, they come from the impact you can have on individual lives. As a teacher, I can testify to the significance of having a student or former student tell me that something I did in class or as a mentor or adviser made a dramatic and positive impact on his or her life. As a writer, I occasionally experience the same thing – a slice of conversation or even a casual comment that suggests that something I wrote made a difference, that it somehow changed a life. As you can imagine, that's very satisfying.

As a leader, you are likely to experience the same reaction to your work, whether in the community or beyond. Hopefully, the problems you help solve, the policies you help design and implement, the technical or artistic advances you facilitate will improve the lives of many individuals, and you will find them grateful for what you have done. If you lead with humility, generosity, and compassion, people will be touched, not only by what you do, but also by who you are.

Beyond the products or policies you affect, you will have the opportunity to work with many different people, and open up new possibilities or just provide needed support for them. You may be able to offer insight and encouragement for them to take on a new project, a new career, or just a new way of working within their current environment. You may say just the right word of encouragement to help them "be all they can be" (but try to do that without using clichés).

It's amazing how a leader's casual comment, even if unintended can open up new doors for another. But those acts of encouragement need not be by chance. Indeed, as a leader, you should always be attentive to doing and saying those things that will encourage others to grow and to lead. It seems such a small thing, but a small thing can make a great difference. Consider, if you will, those turning points or moments of redirection in your life. Not all by any means will have been the result of an act of leadership, but many will, and you will remember those vividly. (This would be a nice moment to reflect on some of those who have made a difference in your own life and to say thank you!)

And remember that you lead not only by what you say and by what you do but by who you are. People watch those who lead carefully, usually looking for clues as to the direction of the group or organization. But in doing so, they also see, evaluate, and may come to emulate the character of the leader, especially a leader for whom they have great respect. If your leadership is based on such enduring qualities as integrity and engagement, those qualities will be spread among others. And while you may not even know what happened, the lives of others will be changed forever – in a good way.

And, importantly, your actions may encourage others to lead. Leadership is not a zero-sum game, the more leadership we can encourage the better off we'll be. I remember an excerpt from *The Merchant of Venice* in which Shakespeare writes,

> The quality of mercy is not strained;
> It droppeth as the gentle rain from heaven
> Upon the place beneath. It is twice blest;
> It blesseth him that gives and him that takes:

I think you'll find that the new leadership we are talking about blesses both the one who leads and the one who is led. I like the quotation here substituting the word "leadership" for "mercy."

> The quality of leadership is not strained;
> It droppeth as the gentle rain from heaven
> Upon the place beneath. It is twice blest;
> It blesseth the one that gives and the one that takes:

Third, the rewards of leadership are many and are expressed both in the impact of the work that you do and in the impact you have on the lives of others. Surprisingly, though, the greatest gift may be the one you receive yourself. Leading will change you as you are challenged and as you grow. You'll never learn as much about yourself as you learn from leading others!

Earlier, I talked about personal energy, social energy, and moral energy. Personal energy is manifest in the leader's self-confidence, self-esteem, persistence, discipline, patience, and tolerance (among other qualities). Social energy is manifest in engagement and the articulation of meaning. Moral energy is manifest in the capacity to apply moral imagination in emerging situations of value conflict. These are just some of the qualities that leaders who are called to energize groups and organizations must demonstrate. If this is the case, then work on your leadership is at the same time work on yourself and vice versa. It is a process, not only of building skills and perspectives, but of building character and commitment.

In the case of the leader, these processes are writ large: they are public, they are direct, and they are transparent. Though the leader may occasionally be shielded from the truth by overzealous followers, a thoughtful and self-reflective leader knows how to take information and experience and turn them into personal growth and self-expression.

As I said earlier, we are at a turning point with respect to leadership, and the way that you lead over the next decades will likely set a pattern for leadership for decades, perhaps even centuries beyond. You can model the old leadership, based on an outdated and incomplete view of human interactions, one dependent on using power-as-coercion. Or you can model a new leadership, one grounded in empathy and imagination, genuine human relationships, and a turn toward the power of expression and collaboration.

As you lead, you will also model a new person-hood. The act of leading will lead you to question yourself and question others, but you will be able to answer those questions from a position of maturity and strength. And at whatever place you find yourself, you will be a better person for having led – whether for a moment, for a period of years, or for a lifetime.

Yours,

Bob

32

LETTER FROM KAYLA

June 1

Bob

I just realized that my last couple of letters were very much focused on the issues you've been raising in your letters. But there have been some interesting things going on in our organization that I'd like to share with you.

A few weeks ago, I was asked to lead a project team working with a local government here in the Los Angeles area. (This is the one I mentioned early on – the contract finally came through.) Our assignment was to help that government conceptualize a new Civic Center, one that would provide a focus for citizen engagement in community affairs, but also conceivably house some programs from Parks and Recreation, some from the library system, and some from Human Services. We were asked to design this project to serve citizens more effectively, to consolidate programs, and to come up with cutting-edge solutions for what has been an historic lack of cooperation among the various agencies.

I don't want to go into detail about the way we have addressed these questions, but I do want to share with you my thoughts about leading the group. As you might guess, I am the youngest of all the members of the project team and younger than most of the local government department heads with whom we'll be working. While I was flattered by being asked to head the team, I was more than a little intimidated – no surprise there, right?

Robert correctly sensed that this might be the case and asked me to visit him in his office before we got started. Even though I feel like I know Robert well, the appointment alone was a little intimidating. But he quickly put me at ease by asking about my family and then asking about you. (Greetings, by the way.) He told me that he had been watching my work from a distance and had been impressed with what I was doing. He said that he had always thought that I should be on the fast track for advancement, and that an opportunity had come up that he thought would provide an excellent leadership experience for me.

Reading between the lines, I translated "experience" to "test," almost thinking of Robert of being "out to get me." This is something I do often, and something I later discussed with Brenda, who has come on board as my leadership coach. Robert is the last person that I would think would be "out to get me," and yet I toyed with exactly that reaction to his assignment for me. As Brenda and I discussed it later, there really wasn't anything in the conversation that supported that interpretation, but that's where I went.

In any case, Brenda said that she recognized that pattern, particularly among young women leaders, and that she felt I was creating an unnecessary roadblock to my own success. My rational self agreed with her, but my insides were still churning. Maybe decades of discrimination have led many women to interpret some things in terms of exploitation and discrimination even when there's no reason to do so. (There certainly are enough real reasons for us to expect discrimination without adding our own self-imposed discrimination to the list.)

But, after some discussion, I agreed to keep notes, to write a journal about my experiences with this project, hoping the journaling would help me clarify the pressures I was facing (or imagining) as I moved into the new assignment.

I won't bore you with the details of the project, but the first thing I did was to assign elements of the project to each of the team members. I asked that they not contact the relevant department heads directly, but that, in order not to confuse our communications, I be involved in all the conversations with them. I even gave the group a little motivational speech about the importance of this project to me and to each of us.

Guess what? After a week or ten days, three of the team members had come to me asking that I "lighten up." One, I later found out, had even written a short note to Robert expressing concerns about my leadership. There were rumors that some of the local department heads were also concerned that Robert had appointed such a young and inexperienced person to lead the team. I am scheduled to see Robert next Friday.

And, frankly, I am scared to death!

Kayla

33
LETTER FROM BOB
June 8

Kayla and Mike,

I haven't received a note from Mike yet, but I thought I would go ahead and write anyway. I'm guessing he's very busy negotiating with the social services agency, and probably equally busy talking with friends and family about the decision. I hope what I'm about to say in this letter helps a little bit.

But before I get into that, Kayla, I wanted to let Mike know that you and I have had a couple of phone calls to discuss your work with the project team. Best of luck in your meeting with Robert. Stay confident, don't get defensive, and be open to learning and change.

Both of you have mentioned your quest for finding meaning in the work you're doing and in the leadership to which you aspire. In thinking about this effort, the word "calling" keeps coming to mind. In part, finding your calling means finding the work you were meant to do. In a larger context, it is about finding the life commitments you wish to make. (I'm not even sure you can separate the two, though most people do.) Identifying your larger calling is complex, involving not just what excites you but what you are ready to commit yourself to morally and ethically. It involves establishing your character as a person and as a leader.

Unfortunately, the popular response to the question of calling focuses on finding the right work and approaching this question in terms of "career advice." How can you succeed in moving up the ladder — assuming you have chosen the right ladder? Here, let's focus on the broader notion of calling, your life's calling. But before we can get to that, we should clear out some underbrush.

There's a lot of talk these days about finding a "passion" and sticking with it throughout your life. Some would say you should simply identify your passion, whatever turns you on day to day and year to year, and then focus exclusively on pursuing that passion. But identifying your passion is neither easy nor perhaps even wise, especially early on. Why should we expect someone with little experience to know what he or she wants to pursue for the rest of his or her life? Some do; most don't. That's a decision that requires maturity and wisdom, sometimes even the wisdom of decades. Passions also change. What you are passionate about at 20 may be quite different from what you are passionate about at 50.

Even if we can identify our passions (which is hard enough), pursuing those passions as a part of our career may not be so easy. Many find themselves in jobs that provide limited opportunities for self-expression, much less passion. And for many that's OK – you may be willing to work in meaningless jobs to have enough money to pursue passions completely outside work.

Others are left searching for the quick self-discovery, the passion that the self-help gurus recommend (either at work or elsewhere), and often feeling guilty because they can't figure it out.

What's more, many people don't recognize their passion until they have achieved it. They go through life following many interests and opportunities, only later recognizing the central thread that held it all together. In his well-known Stanford commencement address in 2005, Steve Jobs put it this way: "You can't connect the dots looking forward; you can only connect them looking backwards."

So, you have to trust that the dots will somehow connect in your future. The Nashville Bluegrass Band is even more to the point: "When I get where I'm goin', that's when I'll know where I'm bound."

Additionally, the find-your-passion advice can morph into a rationalized process of personal goal-setting, especially as passions are translated into specific goals and objectives. Where do I want to be in ten years? What are the steps that will get me there? What are the metrics that I can use to measure my progress? I think these are ticklish questions because they tend to restrict the possibilities for one's life. They suggest a rational/logical process of goal-setting, which, for many, results in a narrowly defined goal. The rational/logical process, of course, fits with and encourages a rational/logical personality. I would suggest that you not over-rationalize the process called "life," which is sterile indeed without emotion, intuition, and beauty.

Finally, the word "passion" carries a somewhat whimsical, fleeting character. It's here today, gone tomorrow, and often formed without any basis in ethics or values. It's built around an individual's own personal interests and may or may not build or contribute to the larger community. It's just not as powerful or enduring as purpose, direction, or commitment. For this reason, I would suggest that, instead of passion, you focus on a personal sense of purpose. By that I mean this: an intent based on your values, one to which you commit yourself fully and show the patience, persistence, drive, and determination to stay with, at least until a better path comes along. Fill in the blank: "I exist to . . ."

As a leader, you may also be expected to articulate a group or organizational sense of purpose, which should be defined in the same way as above and point to a direction based on the values of your group, one to which you commit yourself fully, at least until a better path comes along. Fill in the blank: "Our organization exists to . . ."

Should your personal sense of purpose be the same as your organizational direction and vice versa? Some say yes because both require a value choice, and your values should be consistent. Some say no because you need a life outside work. I would merely say that the two must not be incompatible. If they are, I'd say it's time to find a different line of work. Personal purpose and values take precedence over organizational purpose and values.

All of this is not to say that leaders should be dispassionate. Indeed, passion in pursuit of one's purpose is a virtue (if that passion is not blinded by ego). If you choose to lead, perhaps the most fitting purpose is to integrate, to focus, and to give life to the many separate and often conflicting purposes and passions that dwell in any group, organization, community, or society. And that is something a good leader can and will be both purposeful and passionate about.

Putting Your Journey in Context

Let's next put your leadership journey in a social and moral context. The changes we've been talking about – changes in leadership and organization, changes in technology and the economy, changes in the relationship between work and life outside work, and changes in the way we define happiness – are in many ways liberating. At the same time, they have led to confusion as well. These changes have, in some ways, made it more difficult for you to decide on a path where you can make a significant difference.

- You have more information at your disposal than ever before, yet no one has figured out how to best process that information for the good of humanity.
- You have a wider range of career opportunities than ever before, yet finding a calling that is truly meaningful and purposeful may be more difficult than ever.
- You have more choices than any generation prior to yours, yet settling on a life path that combines meaning, purpose, and balance is still a challenge.

I want to address the question of getting the most out of your development as a leader and as an individual – that is, how to choose a path that is both engaging and meaningful. But it's complicated. "Engaging" is easily understood: you want to do things that capture your imagination and compel your interest. But the word "meaningful" complicates matters because it implies that the choice you face is in part a moral choice – which I believe it is.

In the realm of values, we encounter not only the best leadership has to offer, but also its potentially dark side, the possibility that leadership may be used for deceit and manipulation. Parker Palmer has written, "A leader is someone with the power to project either shadow or light upon some part of the world, and upon the lives of the people who dwell there. A leader shapes the ethos in which others must live, an ethos as light-filled as heaven or as shadowy as hell. A good leader has a high awareness of the interplay of inner shadow and light, lest the act of leadership do more harm than good."

I'm convinced that there are no easy guides for the potential leader. Moral leadership is not based on a set of principles or rules that you can choose to follow or ignore. Human interactions are far too complex for that to work. As much as we have tried over the past hundreds of years to construct rules or codes of conduct, the ethical choices we face are always too difficult for the rules to readily fit all situations and all circumstances. After all, situations change as the cultural circumstances within which we operate differ.

The first step is identifying and framing moral issues, something that requires moral imagination − not only a good sense of ethical awareness, but also the imagination to frame, to articulate, and to act on moral questions. Moral imagination involves, not just a heightened sensitivity to moral concerns, but also careful and thoughtful understanding and evaluation of various options from an ethical standpoint. Acting with moral imagination requires expanding our capacity for moral reasoning and charting new directions for moral action.

Recall my earlier statement that the motives or intentions of the leader are critical to evaluating the ethics of leadership. At the most obvious level, leaders who act in their own self-interest are on dubious moral ground, while those acting in the interest of their followers, or, more generally, the interests of the larger community, are taking the high road.

But the choices you make about your life and your leadership are much more complex, and require some serious soul-searching. Discovering the commitments that you are willing to make is an exercise in personal transformation. Unfortunately, transformation is almost always preceded by hardship, adversity, and trial. But confronting and conquering the demon is essential.

You may be familiar with the ancient and recurring myth of the hero, detailed by Joseph Campbell. The myth is a story told in many different variations throughout history and throughout cultures, but it always follows the same pattern: the adventurer goes forth into the world to encounter unbelievable challenges but eventually conquers the adversary and returns home a hero, transformed by the experience. Sometimes, the battle is with a dragon or other monster that must be slayed; sometimes the battle is with a demon inside. But in any case, you must conquer the villain, and as you do, you will find yourself transformed by the experience.

For our purposes, no battle is more important to leadership than the battle for one's self. Working with one's self is harder by far than working with others.

To succeed in this work is to conquer your fears (including those you don't even know you have), to drive away suffering and despair, and to point your life in the direction of meaning and purpose. The highest human achievement is to elevate one's personal identity, to build an integrated self, and to demonstrate an insurmountable strength of character.

Leadership, then, is about community and relationships, but it is also about character and individual expression. Remember that these choices are not just "feel-good" preferences but are cut through with values. They involve both what to do and how to do it. They must be built on a strong foundation, and each must be consistent with the other. We talk a lot about happiness today and typically measure our passion in terms of the happiness its pursuit brings us. But many people would rather do good deeds even though it might mean less happiness.

Take, for example, a former Miss America, Jackie Mayer, who at age 28 awoke to find herself paralyzed and unable to speak, the victim of a massive stroke. Slowly, she learned to walk again and to speak in sentences, then paragraphs, then entire speeches. Now she inspires others with her message: "It's not the pursuit of happiness that matters, it's the pursuit of significance." A good lesson for all of us.

Remember that the work you do is only a portion of the life you lead. Rather than thinking of the issue in terms of choosing a vocation, think in terms of choosing your life commitments. Answering that question will be difficult – terribly difficult. In part, it is difficult because we don't have clear criteria for evaluating one commitment versus another, nor even clear criteria for evaluating one criterion versus another. It's also difficult because life commitments require an answer, not only to what we are doing but to who we are becoming. (This raises that interesting question about the relationship between the present self and the future self – how should you prepare today for a future self who may have completely different interests from your current self, and why would you?). In any case, to the extent that you can develop some clarity about your broader commitments, the choice of a line of work, a choice of a life direction, or a set of "'becomings" will be much easier.

Two things to guard against: don't make the choice based on the lives of others, and don't make the choice based on what others expect of you. You are not Tim Cook: don't try to imitate him. You are not Oprah Winfrey: don't try to imitate her. Most importantly, don't let the expectations of others make your choice for you. There are many folks that will try to write your life story, but you must not allow them to do so. When people try to tell you who they are, listen carefully. But when people try to tell you who you are, politely turn and walk away.

Admittedly, this advice is easy to give. And it's much easier to follow if you have the financial security that allows you to experiment with different choices. But for many people, locked in low-paying jobs with limited opportunities for career advancement, much less career change, the "passion" advice (and much of my own) rings hollow. I would hope that a change in leadership and in the way we organize would help with this concern, especially as we aim for pay equity, and environmental as well as financial sustainability. Obviously much more is needed. But one thing that is clearly needed is leadership on behalf of social and economic reform.

Meanwhile, one way to resist simply playing out the roles others prescribe for us is to place limits on the intrusion of our jobs and careers into our personal lives. The term work – life balance is often used to characterize the desired outcome, but I'm not sure that term is the correct one.

First, the term separates our existence into two realms, work and everything else (which is called life). I suspect we could easily think of more nuanced ways of describing the many activities that we undertake outside work. Moreover, in most other context, life is the more overarching term. Work is a part of life.

Second, the idea of balance suggests that half of our conscious attention should be focused on work and half on everything else. There may be people who will want to devote more of their attention to work – I guess I'm a prime example. But there also may be people who want to focus very little attention on work and far more on other pursuits. The term "balance" doesn't offer that choice.

I think your generation is more likely than mine to encourage people to develop their own purposes and directions and then find the appropriate settings in which they might best pursue those interests, with the hope that their life will be balanced, coherent, and well-integrated.

I suspect that whatever route you choose, if you make the choice yourself, you will travel that route with more energy and enthusiasm than if someone else says to you, "Travel this road." The oft-heard advice to find your passion at least needs the following emphasis: find *your* passion.

In any case, remember that your choice of a line of work must be framed by your choice of personal commitments, including your commitments to others. And that choice should be informed by the others to whom you are committed. Ultimately, that choice rests on your most cherished values. It is a matter of character, and if you choose to lead, nothing is more important to you than your character. Jobs and opportunities may come and go. But the quality of your character will see you through. Leadership projects who you are in the context of the world around you.

Make your choice of a calling a commitment to character.

Yours,

Bob

34
LETTER FROM MIKE
June 21

Bob

Let me begin by apologizing for my tardiness in responding to your earlier letter, but I was so completely wrapped up in conversations about the social services job that I simply couldn't find time to (or forgot to) write the letter I owed you.

I understand your argument against equating leadership and executive management and the limitations that puts on a person who would lead. I understand the damage this view of leadership in organizations has done and the ethical problems it presents. I have already commented on your discussion of purpose and direction, relationships versus transactions, and the new skills of leadership – and while I have some reservations, mostly about whether you're going too far, I get it.

But the last couple of letters have really felt like they were aimed directly at me. They even caused me to go back and reread some of the earlier letters where we were talking about the leader within. I say that because, as you know, my main concern through our discussions has been how I can find meaning, a sense of personal identity and commitment, in the work that I do and in the leadership I express?

I had been thinking of the old leadership and the new leadership in terms of how we would get things done, and I suppose that's only natural, given the strong cultural emphasis on that way of viewing the world and our place in it. Sometime early on, you mentioned the difference between the head and the heart, which I took to mean the difference between the rational and the emotional/intuitive aspects of our being. It made sense to me that the old leadership and the old way of organizing were primarily dependent on rational processes, while the new leadership and the new way of organizing seem more dependent on emotional/intuitive processes.

But still there was a tension between the two. I saw them as a zero-sum game, and consequently asked whether you thought the emotional, intuitive side would ever come to dominate. But your discussion of character and commitment – the letter where you talked about craftsmanship and sportsmanship, etc. – made me realize that these different aspects of leadership need to be reconciled or integrated deep in our being, and that those aspects are constantly changing, and indeed, they must change, which is the importance of "becoming."

As I think further about this, that's in the same argument you were making about Jung's idea of individuation. First you must separate out the different components of your life and your personality and identify their distinct contributions. Only then can you begin to integrate them, which is the real issue. In terms of leadership, I guess you were saying that it's important to identify the distinct contributions of both the rational and the emotional/intuitive, and then see if you can resolve the tensions between the two, making them whole in your own life, whether doing, being, or becoming.

I think I was putting the pieces together at this point, but you still hadn't convinced me that such a view of leadership would ever be possible, given the power that top executives wield. But then you discussed power-as-coercion and power-as-capacity. And I felt a little light in my head come on.

I may be completely wrong about this, but it seems to me that power-as-capacity is the big picture, organizational-level equivalent of the leader within at the personal level.

My feeling now is that it's very hard to find meaning in your life when you spend most of that life subject to the power of others. Power-as-coercion makes it very hard to find your own sense of meaning, but power-as-capacity is all about meaning. It has to do with building your own life, choosing the directions that you want to pursue, engaging others in an imaginative and constructive way, and working together in building a real sense of caring and community, in yourself and among those around you. As I think about it this way, power-as-capacity is really all about the new leadership, isn't it?

Mike

35

LETTER FROM KAYLA

July 3

Bob

I appreciate your personal note and phone calls just after my last letter. As you know, I was really at a low point and your encouragement helped a lot, as did Mike's texts. But I was still petrified as I thought about my meeting with Robert a few days later. Though I consider Robert a friend and a supporter, even a mentor, I knew things weren't going well for me, and I was sure that I was going to be taken off the project team if not fired outright. After all, he is the CEO and expects top-level performance from his employees.

My anxiety was at an all-time high as I walked into the meeting and found both Robert and Brenda, my executive coach. But Robert was very cordial and asked Brenda and me to join him at a large round table in his office. Robert began by asking a series of questions about the team and my work. I tried to answer as thoroughly and honestly as I could, but I'm sure a little defensiveness crept into what I was saying. With each question I felt that I was painting myself as both incompetent and a real control freak.

Brenda then turned the conversation to how young leaders need to relate to older employees and clients. She pointed out that each age group had to adapt to the other's style, even dropping the dreaded M word, "millennial," to emphasize the differences that had to be overcome. She pointed out that when leaders of all ages feel that they are under pressure they tend to revert to the traditional command-and-control approach to management and leadership. That sure sounded like me.

What was most interesting was that everything that was said to me echoed things that I had said about other leaders in the organization, particularly those senior managers that I accused earlier of being disrespectful. A few weeks earlier, I could not have imagined that those same complaints would be directed at me. But there they were.

Robert and Brenda then gave me some pointers on stress reduction techniques as well as ways to create common ground among members of the team and between the team and the department heads. I could hardly believe what was happening – they were going to give me a second chance!

I left feeling relieved, but recognized I had a lot of work to do – on myself. In fact, Robert said as much as he closed the meeting. I could almost hear your voice echoing in the background as he talked about the importance of building one's own character and personal skills (relationships? squishy skills?) before trying to lead others. Even more important than what he was saying was the fact that he himself exhibited such quiet confidence in everything he did. His words were important, but his model was even more so.

It's now almost a month later and I must admit things are going much, much better. I'm feeling calmer and more self-assured and I think that carries over to the rest of the team. What have I learned from all this? One thing is that if you are experiencing tension in a situation, it's likely to be reflected in your approach to others who are involved. You want to be calm, but you don't want to be so calm that you miss things. You need to maintain sufficient focus on the work to take in the information that you need. But there's a line between focused and panicky that you can't cross.

Oh yes! One more thing! As fate, or perhaps Robert would have it, one of my project team members, the one who had complained about my being assigned to lead the project was the same sexist Howard Clark who had ordered me to get coffee for him months and months ago. This time, before he even got settled, I said, "Mr. Clark, would you please join me in getting coffee for everyone before we begin?" His first reaction was an almost imperceptible grimace, but then, as if a revelation had washed over him, he smiled and said to me, with a wink, "I'd be delighted to." For the first time, I think he really got it – or maybe he was just pulling my leg from the beginning. In any case, from that point forward, he and I have been not quite "good buddies," but at least cordial. I guess sometimes you can make a difference – maybe just one sexist at a time, but you can make a difference.

I remember a line from your little red book, *Just Plain Good Management*, when you were talking about "dealing with jerks." You said, "Recovering jerks can actually become your strongest allies." It's hard to think of Howard Clark as an ally, but he and I are moving in that direction. He's really a lot smarter than I realized. I guess you need to be ready for lots of surprises in this world!

One more thing. This whole experience has really had a huge impact on me. I think I'm more careful in my interactions with others, but I'm also much more confident in working with others. I know now that I can work effectively with many different types of people and I can even lead people effectively. I realize that self-confidence can morph into excessive ego so I must be careful of that, but the quiet confidence I've seen in you and in Robert has become a "north star." Bob, I'm really pleased with how far I've come on the path to leadership. And it was all triggered by focusing on the leader within!

Kayla

36

LETTER FROM MIKE

July 16

Bob

    I have news. I accepted the social services offer and will start the first of next month!

    I want to thank you and Kayla for your help. Certainly, your comments about "calling" weighed heavily in my decision. When Annie and I started thinking of the position, not just in terms of a job, but as an opportunity for me to lead, to serve, and to cultivate meaning in my own life and the lives of others, the decision became much clearer. And Kayla's steady barrage of encouraging texts kept me focused and positive about it all!

    I know the new job will be challenging, not only as I try to clarify the purpose and direction of the organization and establish good relationships with our employees, our clients, and our many stakeholders, but as I help build the narrative of the group so that we can reach our full potential in service to the community. And yes, I'll be looking for that "Leadership Moment," and when it occurs I'll be sure to let you know.

    Notice I said, "when it occurs" rather than "if it occurs." I can do this. I'm now on a meaningful path, a path of service to the community, and a path to a new and invigorated sense of leadership. I know why I want to lead and how I want to lead, and that really feels good.

    What is most apparent is that my choice reflected a desire to experiment with a new leadership, the one we've been building throughout these letters. But what brought it all together was my realizing that the new leadership we have been discussing can't be achieved without a deep personal commitment. The new leadership for a new generation must grow from the inside out!

Letter from Mike July 16

Well, I'm so excited now that I can't write anymore. But I hope you will accept my invitation to come visit and have a glass of champagne to celebrate. After all, you're implicated in all of this. I've come a long way in the last few months, and I appreciate all that you've done to help define the path I'm on. Of course, if anything goes wrong, I'm holding you responsible!

Mike

37
LETTER FROM BOB
July 18

Dear Kayla and Mike,

I'm so pleased that you both seem to have reached a new plateau in your personal approach to leadership. You have correctly identified some of the most significant issues that you will face in your leadership journey. You understand the emotional, relational, and ethical dimensions of leadership. And you have a good sense of how these will affect your life overall.

Given this reading of your situation, I want to congratulate you for reaching so far, albeit through some personal struggle and considerable self-reflection. You seem confident that you can do the work required in the next position, and I don't think there was ever any doubt about that. But you also seem more confident that you can lead in your company, and do so in a way that provides meaning to the organization and meaning to you.

Doing so may require some reshaping of what people expect from someone in your position – that is, they will need to learn that your approach to leadership will be different from the traditional approach. And that may take some time. But I think you're ready for that. Congratulations again!

Oh, and lest we forget, congratulations also on the "late-breaking news" that you, Kayla, are having a child, your first! I know that you and your husband will find parenthood one of the most demanding, challenging, exacting, troubling, distressing, maddening, infuriating . . . You will find it one of the best experiences of your life!

Of course, having a child will impact your work in some obvious ways. You will have to deal with issues of maternity leave, child care, and the interplay of life and work. But being a parent will also influence your leadership in subtler ways. In fact, you should prepare your leadership psyche for a real shake-up as you try to exercise leadership at home over the coming years. One suggestion: you will learn as much or more about leadership from watching your child lead you as you will from watching you and your husband trying to lead your child. You will easily see how you energize your child, but it will be more worthwhile to you as a leader to observe and understand how your child energizes you. Prepare to be led as well as to lead. I said earlier that learning to lead requires learning to learn. You have just signed on to leadership lessons for a lifetime!

And Mike, congratulations to you as well! I'm sure that your new position will be not only rewarding day to day but will give you the opportunity to lead in both the organization and the community. I also must congratulate you on your choice of service to others – that is, finding work in which you will make a meaningful contribution to your community.

I also think that you and your family made a good choice with respect to Annie's future aspirations as a poet and the opportunities your kids will have to grow and flourish within a highly supportive environment. It must have been especially nice to have your community of friends and neighbors interested in what you and Annie were going to do and, at the same time, being supportive of your choice, whatever that might be. But I know they are glad you will still be around.

I must confess now that when you first mentioned the new opportunity with the nonprofit, I was hesitant to assert my opinion too strongly. But I have to say that I thought this job was right for you. It provides an opportunity for you to contribute, to grow, and to lead. I'm glad you made the choice you did. You chose the pursuit of significance!

And I know you join me in congratulating Kayla as she and her husband enter the confusing and complex but wonderful world of parenthood. It occurs to me, somewhat ironically, that you have some experience and probably some advice to pass on to Kayla about her home life – after all, you and Annie have young children yourselves. But Kayla may have some experience and advice to pass on to you and other men about moving from old stereotypes to new levels of maturity and self-confidence as a leader. Her journey over the past several months, like yours, has been one of self-reflection leading to personal change. Being able to challenge yourself and to conquer your personal fears, however big or small, is a key to becoming a leader. And both of you seem well along that path.

And speaking of paths, isn't it ironic that we near the end of our discussion talking about paths. This is where we started. In your first letter, Kayla, you talked about your "path to leadership" and, Mike, you described yourself as being on a "path to self-discovery." To my mind, those paths are really one and the same. And what progress you both have made!

Yours,

Bob

38
LETTER FROM BOB
July 21

Dear Kayla and Mike,

I'd like to use this final letter to express my sincere appreciation for your help in this project, and my excitement about where you're heading, and to issue a challenge to others who will follow in your path. I want to speak to the personal experience of leadership.

Throughout our letters, you and I talked about the rapid changes affecting our societies, our organizations, and our leadership. We saw social and economic shifts caused by globalization, we saw dramatic changes in the way communications occur in the digital world, and we saw rising expectations for work and the demand for greater autonomy and purpose in the workplace (and elsewhere).

There is no reason to think these trends will not continue, unless we experience a cataclysmic environmental disaster or a global collapse of social and economic institutions – neither of which is out of the question. But taking the more hopeful view – that we survive – we can expect rapid change to continue to affect every aspect of our physical, social, and economic world. Under these circumstances, leaders and leadership will constantly be under pressure to change as well.

As you recall, one variation of the old leadership was "situational leadership." Its proponents argued that managers needed to shift their "styles" according to the type of organization they were heading. The manager of a social services agency might take one approach, one more relationship-oriented, while the manager of a police department might take another, one more structured and task-oriented. The theory made some sense in the abstract. But the practical recommendation that came from that (that leaders need to adapt their styles to different situations) was misleading.

We don't come into an organization saying, "I'm going to choose this leadership style for the next hour and then shift back to another for the rest of the afternoon." The experience of leadership, the flow of leadership from day to day, the pace at which we work simply doesn't allow that kind of thinking.

Yes, leadership does require adaptability. But adaptability must be a part of your core being, not a superficial variation of a personality that changes from day to day and organization to organization. If you try to act out the recommended style (emphasis on the "act out"), you are most likely to appear inauthentic, or "play-acting" at best and simply lost and confused at worst. Leadership is not acting. It must be real.

In any case, the differences in types of organizations are already less significant than the differences in social and cultural norms. We easily recognize this phenomenon across national boundaries, where expectations of leaders vary considerably. We also saw these differences at play in our discussion of the cultural expectations of men and women in the workplace. But I think you need to be aware of even more subtle changes. People will develop different interests and expectations from year to year, month to month, even day to day. For this reason, as a leader you will need to be fully attentive to shifts in the societies and cultures of which you are a part and with which you interact.

The term "cultural awareness," as it is used today, means an awareness of and sensitivity to race, ethnicity, gender, and sexual orientation. That's very important, but in addition, I would recommend your being aware of all the subtle and not-so-subtle cultural shifts that are occurring in the time and place where you live. These shifts will affect the expectations people have for you and other leaders, and they will affect you as well.

At one cultural moment or place, people will seek leaders to bring big ideas to the front. They will expect their leaders to be active and assertive. At other times and in other places, they will need leaders who allow them time to pause and reflect. They will expect their leaders to play a much more passive and supportive role. In either case, they will rebel against leaders who push too hard for change or those who seem too timid for the times. They will dismiss leaders who misread the suitability of their approach for the times in which they live.

The symbols and artifacts of a cultural moment will affect the cues you pick up on and the signals and images you will use in turn to communicate with others. Even the images and sounds of pop culture (that, as you know, I sometimes indulge, sometimes embrace, and sometimes even obsess over!) are among the cultural shifts that will affect your leadership.

The key for you is to develop a comprehensive understanding of the society and culture in which you operate. You must develop a "cultural radar" that allows you to pick up on the slightest shifts in the ideas and expectations that guide people. You must be attentive not only to cultural "waves" but also to cultural conflicts, both of which may reveal themselves dramatically or with quiet subtlety.

You will need to carefully consider ideas and explorations; to engage with the creative world, including art, music, and dance; to recognize the emergence and decline of cultural icons from athletics to entertainment; to be sensitive to the casual conversation before the movie starts as well as the depths of wisdom and spirituality in the film.

You must play an active role in interacting with the social and cultural world. Your intelligence, imagination, and energy must come into play in sorting out what's consequential and what's tangential. Your creativity will be put to the test as you work through wildly divergent ideas and as those begin to converge. And after shifting through the many grains of cultural sand, you will need the social and cultural awareness to articulate the narrative of the group in its most elegant and meaningful expression.

As a leader, you will take complex material and make it simple and understandable. That is not to say that it will be simplistic; it will be the essential. You will extract what is most significant and communicate it in a way that makes sense to others. The leader goes to the essence of the matter.

In large part, your strength as a leader must be based on your capacity for the creative. You must be able to absorb diversity and complexity, to synthesize different ideas, and to articulate the core of any matter in a clear and meaningful fashion.

Doing so is not merely an exercise in rational thinking. Chester Barnard, business executive and management theorist, put it well nearly 75 years ago when he wrote that, for leaders, the essential capability is "the sensing of the organization as a whole and the total situation relevant to it. It transcends the capacity of merely intellectual methods. . . . The terms pertinent to it are feeling, judgment, sense, proportion, balance, appropriateness. It is a matter of art rather than science, and it is aesthetic rather than logical."

It requires a special ability to look at the vast sea of data and information the environment presents, then pick out only the most relevant cues and information. You must organize those ideas and aspirations into a framework that can be easily communicated and that will make sense to potential followers. You must then present your ideas in ways that are meaningful and compelling.

And, importantly, we should remember that these cultural trends don't just shape the culture within which you will lead – they shape your own identity. So, the leader must carefully look inside as well as outside, sorting out the significant messages from the cultural "noise."

The Art of Leadership

This is what I mean when I talk about the art of leadership. As you know, I have always considered the arts integrally related to leadership. The arts can sharpen our sensibilities, especially our capacity to find beauty and significance in the world around us. The arts can help model and stimulate both the skills and perspective that leaders need. And the arts can lead, changing the way that we view the world and changing the meaning that we draw from our relationships with others. Let's look at each of these connections.

First, the arts can enhance our capacity for recognizing beauty and meaning. Remember that the leader brings special insight to the process of building a group's or organization's narrative. The leader doesn't just react to the group's conversation but interacts with the group and contributes to the development of the resulting narrative. The leader's ability to do so depends, in large part, on his or her own capacity for creative insight. In part, insight is built around intellectual ability and practice — reading, analyzing, discussing, and concluding. But the less obvious, though sometimes more important, source of insight is the leader's talent for artistic understanding — that is, reading the images, symbols, and metaphors that help us access the hidden depths of meaning that underlie all our cultural expressions.

This, of course, is both the language and the preoccupation of the artist. The artist draws us into the world of beauty, or at least to those objects that capture our attention and move us deeply. More importantly, the artist points out sometimes disturbing anomalies in our cultural milieu and urges us to act to sort out the difference between what seems important and what really is. For you as a leader, the first step is to enhance your capacity to traverse with confidence the symbolic and metaphorical world that the artist reveals. Engage with the arts — painting, sculpture, music, theater, dance, and the like — and draw from them the clever, astute, and even spiritual sustenance they offer. You will learn about yourself, you will learn about others, and you will learn about leadership.

Second, the arts can also help you develop your leadership skills. You may have seen our book, *The Dance of Leadership*, in which Janet and I employed art, music, and dance as metaphors for leadership. After interviewing artists, musicians, and especially dancers, not about their leadership but about how they approached their disciplines, we identified several lessons that translated easily to the world of leadership.

Leadership, for example, depends on rhythm and timing. A solid rhythm in an organization provides grounding. A steady rhythm is a sign of a good working order; it lets people know there is something regular and predictable they can count on. However, this doesn't mean everyone must operate in the same rhythm. Nor does it mean the rhythm should be mechanical, devoid of breath, spirit, and energy.

Certainly, most people recognize that there are differences in pace or tempo in their organizations from time to time. And indeed, one of the leader's roles is to help set the pace of the organization. For some, that means quickening the pace. In fact, one CEO told us that his job was "to take the organization around the curve as fast as we can go without falling off the cliff."

On the other hand, sometimes a slower pace may make more sense. A corporate VP told Janet and me that the tempo of her group's work had slowed since they moved their division from one company to another. But she said that was a good thing. "The quality of our work has improved. And the quality of our work life has improved."

One skill of the successful leader is the capacity to identify rhythms, to become adept in different rhythms, and to translate across rhythmic boundaries. For example, while a regular beat is important, a leader might want to vary the rhythm of an organization to stimulate creativity and new thinking.

We said, "Leaders connect with others emotionally in a way that energizes them and moves them to act." But, of course, the same could be said of artists. So instead of using art as a metaphor for leadership, I'm now convinced that leadership is an art and that art can lead — which takes us to our next point.

Third, the artist can lead and, in leading, energize groups, organizations, and entire societies. In fact, the leadership provided by the very best artists may be among the most compelling and enduring leadership of all.

We have described the process of leading as one that involves engaging with a group or organization to draw forth and creatively shape the group's narrative and potential. The articulation of that narrative provides the spark that ignites action in the group.

The work of the artist follows the same pattern, though at a scale and a level of both abstractness and concreteness that eludes leaders elsewhere. Typically, the engagement or conversation of the artist is not with a group or organization, but with the broader culture or a significant portion of that culture — for example, the aesthetic, the economic, or the political.

The artist's calling is to reveal the culture's deepest yearnings, its capacities and limitations. Artists, like other leaders, identify patterns and connections that others fail to see, then draw upon their own curiosity, imagination, and creativity to construct a new portrayal of the world through their painting, music, comedy, dance, and so on.

The paradox is that the level of abstraction involved in the artist's engagement with the larger culture is far greater than that of most leaders as they engage with a group or organization. But the resulting artistic product, no matter how esoteric its meaning, is far more visible and concrete than the narrative of most leaders.

In any case, the interpretation of the world contained in a piece of art becomes an alternative cultural narrative. Even the smallest artistic object or combination of notes, sounds, and movements defy convention and compel us to see the world in a different way. Indeed, that is exactly the reason we're drawn to pieces of art: they address our longing to throw off the constraints of everyday life and see life as the miracle and mystery it is.

The artist may take the perspective of the pre-conventional — that is, opening our eyes to the hidden and not previously revealed forces that have led us to the present. This perspective invites us to reconstitute our understanding of the ordinary in our day-to-day lives. But the artist may also take the perspective of the post-conventional — that is, providing us with glimpses of what the future, or better, what alternative futures may hold. This perspective helps us construct our understanding of the possible. The artist leads through comprehension, reflection, and critique of the existing culture, then articulates a new message through the production of artistic products that are so compelling that we must act.

Again, leadership, as we have described it, can be informed by the world of art, can be enhanced by our exposure to art, and, at the very highest level, it is the same as art. Artistic leadership, defined either as leadership informed by art or as the broad cultural leadership that art provides, may be both the most practical and the most empathetic possible. I invite you to engage art and artistry in your daily life; you will be a better leader having done so.

The Soul of Leadership

And what about the soul of leadership, a phrase we used earlier? Certainly, you might say that over the past decades, leadership has been rationalized and mechanized, even merchandized to the point where it has lost its soul. Leadership is no longer about the grand ideas of justice, freedom, and equality. It's no longer about the search for human dignity and human aspiration. It's no longer the province of philosophy or metaphysics. Rather, leadership today is about getting things done in the most efficient and least costly manner possible. It's about productivity and results. It's the same as management.

But I'm not ready to write off the soul of leadership so easily. It may be damaged, but if so, a central part of your leadership journey must be its resurrection.

Thinking about the soul of leadership sent me scurrying to my online dictionary, in which I found three clusters of definitions of soul. The first, which I think of as the conventional sense of the term, is that soul is "the spiritual aspect of human existence, thought to be separate from the body and enduring after death."

Certainly, you hope that the core of what you do as a leader will continue after you have moved on. But it's likely – in fact, almost inevitable – that your successors will try to draw a distinction between your work and theirs. Far too few new leaders try to build explicitly on what came before. Most want to create their own identity and think they must do so by distancing themselves from the past and from their predecessors.

But your acts of leadership will live on, both in the impact you have had on the world and the way in which you have changed leadership itself. As I said before, the history of humankind can be read as a movement from power and domination to freedom and autonomy. I am confident that your leadership will push the frontier of this movement, maybe slightly, maybe dramatically, but in the right direction. Leadership will never be quite the same because of what you do as a leader. You will have advanced the spirit of freedom on Earth and perhaps beyond. That's no small contribution, and it will be a lasting one.

The second set of definitions describes soul as "the emotional part of human nature, the seat of feelings or sentiments; high-mindedness, noble warmth of feeling, spirit or courage." Soul in this sense certainly seems consistent with our description of the "squishy" skills of leadership, especially as we included such qualities as caring, compassion, and love. What's more, in this definition of soul, there is an emphasis on ideals such as wisdom, purpose, and courage. Maybe it is the soul of leadership that urges us as leaders to embrace the most high-minded of human virtues.

In this sense, leading with soul involves touching the spirit of the group or organization in a way that is inspiring and moving. It challenges the leader and the group to seek higher purposes, to create meaningful experiences and relationships, and to impact society in a positive way. As a leader, you have the capacity, even the responsibility to ignite the flame of nobility in the group.

There remains a third set of definitions of soul: "an animating principle, the essential element or part of something; the inspirer, the moving spirit of some action." I can't help but think that this definition of soul is almost identical to the definition of leadership we have discussed over and over in these letters – leadership energizes.

Real leadership is indeed an animating force and represents the spirit of collective action. The act of leading goes beyond profit and productivity to engage and to inspire groups, organizations, communities, and entire societies to their greatest achievements. In the leadership moment, people are called to strive for their highest potential, including the potential for extending the most cherished human values and establishing new arenas for meaningful human action.

Crafting Your Leadership Journey

If the soul of leadership involves the moral and the philosophical, it also involves the aesthetic. Leadership involves creativity, expression, and a commitment to revealing aspects of human life that otherwise remain buried beneath our conscious day-to-day living, but that carry with them the most significant and meaningful elements of our existence. In the world of leadership, the art is not increasing beauty (though it certainly may do so) but expressing human meaning.

The most important artistry associated with your leadership is that of crafting your own leadership journey, which is the art of working on yourself. Leadership is not just a way of doing, or even a way of being, it is a way of becoming. The only way you can become a better leader is to become a better person.

In each step of your leadership journey, you will need to consider the world around you, but you must also draw from within. Your leadership will be born into the complexity of your life experiences, ranging from the practical to the philosophical. It will be enriched by the rays of meaning and significance that you bring to your experiences and those of others. And it will be manifest in the world outside only after you have measured its maturity and value from the inside.

The leadership you bring to a group or organization will be a combination of the intelligence, the skills, and the qualities you possess, combined with the accumulation of thousands of different experiences you have had over your lifetime. For the most part, these experiences will seem unremarkable, but they will in time be evident in their effect on you. At other moments, however, you will know that something significant is happening – a life-changing experience. I suspect you are living in such a period right now.

You bring yourself, shaped by your experience and reflected in what you call your personality. That perspective is not captured by the term "leadership style." In fact, it is exactly the opposite. It's not style. It's not acting. It's substance. Leadership is deeply connected to the person you are inside. It comes from the totality of your skills and values, mediated by the culture and context in which you find yourself.

Remember also that experience doesn't work strictly in words. It operates in images, symbols, and metaphors. And those clusters of meaning can be interpreted reliably only by testing them against the flow of human experiences, your own and those of others. Again, this is the benefit of self-reflection and self-critique – to learn and to grow.

Leadership is an interpretation and projection of your character and your commitment to making the world a better place. You must look carefully inside, sorting out the significant messages from the irrelevant, and resisting the temptation to be the person others want you to be. You must be yourself. But then you must engage in a way that shapes human energy and moves other people to act as well.

Though you will give energy to efforts that will change the world, you must start with what's growing inside. As you confront the world outside, be sure to establish your own "soulful" signature, your own voice, and draw from "the leader within."

Ending? No, beginning!

What is left to be said, except perhaps to pull together some of the threads of advice that have been hidden beneath the surface of my portrayal of leadership, past, present, and future? I expect that some of your friends will lead in corporate and governmental settings, while others will focus their leadership on their families and communities. Others may lead through the arts and the creative disciplines. You too will find your place and time to lead, whether you choose the opportunity or it is thrust upon you by circumstance.

You will spend considerable time developing the traits and skills needed to manage. These will include the hard, the soft, and the squishy skills. The latter, of course, will be particularly valuable to you as a leader. The essence of leadership is to energize.

But the development of skills is not enough. In addition, as a leader, you must have perspective – an understanding of the world, the ability to sort out the meaningful from the mundane, and the inner strength to act on the difference between the two. You don't gain that inner capacity merely by working in the world: you gain it by working with yourself.

A sense of introspection and self-reflection requires focus, concentration, and the ability to select the right idea or the right object to address. Grab a moment – an hour, a day, or a week. Get away, take a walk in the woods, paddle across the lake, listen to your favorite music, or whatever soothes you. Most of all, unplug, at least occasionally. Sometimes you must break your connection with others to improve your connection with others.

Having done so, you may encounter the depths of human consciousness. For indeed, the myths and symbols and metaphors of the ages still haunt our daily lives, stalking our every move, ready to rise up and change our dreams into nightmares. But these very same forces can light our paths and turn those nightmares into problems solved. Just like the hero of ancient myths and legends, you must go forth to confront the demon, the dragon, the monster. You must be up to the challenge, whether physical or psychological or spiritual, and return home victorious and ready to lead.

Memories, dreams, and illusions lie just beneath the surface of our consciousness, waiting to assert their own peculiar versions of reality and falsehood and sometimes to deceive us into following our own ego rather than serving others. But alongside these deceptions lie our curiosity and our imagination, where ideas and images prepare to spring forth as something bold, new, and filled with promise. Somewhere in that mix of melancholy and ideals you will find your distinctive voice, the voice of your leadership. Heed and employ that voice as you engage with yourself, with groups, with organizations, with communities, and with entire societies. Your best and most lasting contributions will be marked by creativity, character, and compassion. They will spring from the innermost reaches of your spirit and your soul.

You and other young leaders hold the future in your hands and in your hearts. Cherish your opportunity to lead and shape the future, starting at whatever level you find yourself. Treat your journey with enthusiasm, with confidence, and with respect. It is a crucial endeavor, an essential journey, and a great responsibility.

The spirit of leadership, the soul of the leader, resides in each of you and the world awaits your story. From here on, the letters to be written are the lives you live and the leadership you give. Start writing!

Yours,

Bob

> You are young. So you know everything. You leap
> into the boat and begin rowing. But, listen to me.
> Without fanfare, without embarrassment, without
> any doubt, I talk directly to your soul. Listen to me.
> Lift the oars from the water, let your arms rest, and
> your heart, and heart's little intelligence, and listen to
> me. There is life without love. It is not worth a bent
> penny, or a scuffed shoe. It is not worth the body of a
> dead dog nine days unburied. When you hear, a mile
> away and still out of sight, the churn of the water
> as it begins to swirl and roil, fretting around the
> sharp rocks – when you hear that unmistakable
> pounding – when you feel the mist on your mouth
> and sense ahead the embattlement, the long falls
> plunging and steaming – then row, row for your life
> toward it.
>
> – Mary Oliver, West Wind

"You are young. So you know everything." from WEST WIND: Poetry and Prose Poems by Mary Oliver. Copyright @ 1997 by Mary Oliver. Reprinted by permission of Houghton Mifflin Harcourt Publishing Company. All rights reserved.

ENDNOTES

Letter 1

. . . you don't understand it well enough." Albert Einstein. Online at https://en.wikiquote.org/wiki/User:Ningauble.

. . . the leader within." Parker Palmer, "Leading from Within," *Let Your Life Speak: Listening for the Voice of Vocation.* John Wiley & Sons, Inc., 2000, Chapter 5. Online at www.couragerenewal.org/parker/writings/leading-from-within/.

Letter 2

. . . respect, and even compassion for others. Robert B. Denhardt, *Just Plain Good Management.* New Insight Press, 2014.

. . . fully integrated human being. Warren Bennis, quoted in Kevin Cashman, "Five Enduring Leadership Lessons." *Forbes*, September 5, 2014. Online at www.forbes.com/sites/kevincashman/2014/09/05/five-enduring-leadership-lessons/#6ca1c8bc600c.

Letter 4

. . . shadow of organization." Robert B. Denhardt, *In the Shadow of Organization.* University Press of Kansas, 1981.

. . . more elastic and more penetrable. Zygmunt Bauman, *Liquid Modernity.* Polity Press, 2000.

. . . fairness, equity, and sustainability. Dave Stangis and Katherine Valvoda Smith, *21st Century Corporate Citizenship.* Emerald Publishing, 2017.

. . . holds over 60 percent. *Federal Reserve Bulletin*, v. 103, no. 3, September 2017. Online at www.federalreserve.gov/publications/files/scf17.pdf.

. . . faster and more durable growth." Jonathan D. Ostry, Andrew Berg, and Charalambos G. Tsangarides, "Redistribution, Inequality, and Growth," IMF Staff Discussion Note. International Monetary Fund, February 2014.

. . . caring, compassion, and love. Robert B. Denhardt, *In the Shadow of Organization*. University Press of Kansas, 1981.

Letter 11

. . . complexity and richness." George Hagman, *Aesthetic Experience*. Rodopi, 2011, p. 71.

. . . their fortunes rise and fall together." James MacGregor Burns, *Leadership*. Harper Torchbooks, 1978, p. 426.

Letter 17

. . . a clarity of ideas and principles." George Will. Online at www.thisdayinquotes.com/2011/01/george-hw-bush-and-vision-thing.html.

. . . until they get punched in the mouth." Mike Tyson. Online at www.brainyquote.com/quotes/mike_tyson_382439.

It will never be the plan." Jeff Bezos, quoted by Erika Andersen, "What Jeff Bezos Knows about Planning vs. Reality," *Forbes*, September 23, 2013. Online at www.forbes.com/sites/erikaandersen/2013/09/23/what-jeff-bezos-knows-about-planning-vs-reality/#80f24892d5b1.

What doesn't change is the "why" of our work. Angela Blanchard, quoted in Anjali Mullany, "Generation Flux Salon," *Fast Company*, November 5, 2012.

. . . to create meaningful futures." Ralph Kerle, "How the Skill of Envisioning Creates Purposeful Futures," July 29, 2014. Online at www.linkedin.com/pulse/20140729230311-1726879-how-the-skill-of-envisioning-creates-purposeful-futures/.

It's about being flexible and consistent at the same time." Angela Blanchard, quoted in Anjali Mullany, "Generation Flux Salon," *Fast Company*, November 5, 2012.

[L]eaders make things simple." Bill Post, CEO, Pinnacle West, Personal interview, 2006.

. . . my core values do not." Dinah Boyd, quoted in Anjali Mullany, "Generation Flux Salon," *Fast Company*, November 5, 2012.

Letter 18

. . . in the interest of more efficient production. Frederick Taylor, *The Principles of Scientific Management* (originally published in 1911). Cosimo Classics, 2010.

. . . repair the wiring. See, for example, Thomas Lewis, Fari Amini, and Richard Lannon, *A General Theory of Love*. Vintage, 2001.

Letter 20

. . . whose name has slipped away. C. G. Jung, *Psychological Types*, 3rd ed. Princeton University Press.

Letter 21

. . . a couple of random examples. Peter Senge, Joseph Jaworski, Otto Scharmer, and Betty Sue Flowers, *Presence*. Society for Organizational Learning, 2004; C. Otto Scharmer, *Theory U: Leading from the Future as it Emerges*. Society for Organizational Learning, 2007.

. . . a process he called "individuation." C. G. Jung, *Symbols of Transformation* (vol. 2). Harper & Brothers, 1962.

. . . the advance of autonomy and freedom. Georg Wilhelm Friedrich Hegel. *Reason in History: A General Introduction to the Philosophy of History*. (originally published in 1824). Liberal Arts Press, 1953.

. . . beyond the existing state of affairs." Herbert Marcuse, "Introduction," *An Essay on Liberation*. Beacon Press, 1971.

. . . realm of freedom." Herbert Marcuse, "Introduction," *An Essay on Liberation*. Beacon Press, 1971.

. . . communications free of domination." Jürgen Habermas, *Knowledge and Human Interests*, Jeremy Shapiro trans. Beacon Press, 1971, p. 93.

. . . transparency is simply wrong. Jeffrey Pfeffer, *Power: Why Some People Have It and Others Don't*. Harper Collins, 2010.

Letter 27

. . . attitudes of white superiority." Peggy C. Davis, "Law as Microaggression," *Yale Law Journal*, 98, 1989, 1559–77.

. . . wearing the same clothes." Reuben Brock, personal communication, 2018.

. . . not too damn talented." Ellen McGirt, "Young, Black, and Left Out of Corporate America," *Fortune*, January 22, 2016. Online at http://fortune.com/video/2016/01/22/leading-while-black/.

. . . even by other women. Jasmin Davidds, personal communication, 2017.

. . . corporate or governmental world. Jasmin Davidds, personal communication, 2017.

. . . loves to go dancing. Marisa Salcines, corporate executive, quoted in Ruchika Tulshyan, "Speaking Up as a Woman of Color at Work," *Forbes*, February 10, 2015. Online at www.forbes.com/sites/ruchikatulshyan/2015/02/10/speaking-up-as-a-woman-of-color-at-work/#57d90ac42ea3/.

Letter 30

. . . fails to explain anomalies. Thomas Kuhn, *The Structure of Scientific Revolutions*, 4th ed. The University of Chicago Press, 2015.

... the classic book *Flatland*? Edwin Abbott, *Flatland* (originally published in 1884). Dover Publications, 2017.

... to symbolically "kill" the leader. Sigmund Freud, Chapter 10 – "The Group and the Primal Horde," *Group Psychology and the Analysis of The Ego* (originally published in 1821). Empire Books, 2011.

... him that gives and him that takes. William Shakespeare, *The Merchant of Venice*, Act 4, Scene 1.

Letter 33

... connect them looking backwards." Steve Jobs, Commencement address, Stanford University, June 12, 2005.

... know where I'm bound." Nashville Bluegrass Band, "When I Get Where I'm Goin'," on album *Waiting for the Hard Times to Go*, Sugar Hill Records, 1993.

... do more harm than good." Parker Palmer, "Leading from Within," *Let Your Life Speak: Listening for the Voice of Vocation*. John Wiley & Sons, Inc., 2000, Chapter 5.

... detailed by Joseph Campbell. Joseph Campbell, *The Hero with a Thousand Faces*. Princeton University Press, 1973.

It's the pursuit of significance." Robert B. Denhardt, *The Pursuit of Significance*. Waveland Press, 2000.

Letter 34

... recovering jerks can become your strongest allies. Robert B. Denhardt, *Just Plain Good Management*. New Insight Publishers, 2014.

Letter 38

... aesthetic rather than logical." Chester I. Barnard, *The Functions of the Executive*. Harvard University Press, 1948, p. 235.

... as metaphors for leadership. Robert B. Denhardt and Janet V. Denhardt, *The Dance of Leadership: The Art of Leading in Business, Government, and Society*. Routledge, 2015.

... falling off the cliff." Robert Johnson, CEO Honeywell Aerospace, personal interview, 2006.

... quality of our work life has improved." Cathy McKee, VP of General Dynamics Decision Systems, personal interview, 2006.

... enduring after death." All definitions online at dictionary.com.

... a variation of "situational leadership." Center for Leadership Studies, Cary, North Carolina. Online at www.situational.com/.

A READER'S GUIDE TO THE LITERATURE ON LEADERSHIP

The literature in the field of leadership is highly diverse, with articles and books that approach the topic from the perspectives of research and scholarship, theory and practice, ethics and philosophy, and practical advice and guidance. For someone just starting out in the study and practice of leadership, the vast array of materials can be intimidating. For this reason, I wanted to include some bibliographic notes that may help focus your reading (I will limit my review to books published in the last 20 years, except to comment on a couple of earlier "classics" with which you should be familiar).

Quick Start

Leadership has been discussed for hundreds, even thousands of years with the early writers focusing on political and military leadership. In the last century, however, leadership studies have become more associated with executive leadership in the corporate and governmental sectors.

For a historical perspective, you might look at Barbara Kellerman's, *Leadership*, an edited volume of commentaries on leadership through the centuries, or you might read *Leadership Matters* by Thomas Cronin and Eugene Genovese, especially the chapters on what the classics teach us.

There are several excellent texts providing overviews of the study and practice of leadership. Among these I think you would find any one of these useful: *Leadership: Theory and Practice* or *An Introduction to Leadership: Concepts and Practice*, both by Peter Northouse, *Leadership in Organizations* by Gary Yukl, and *Leadership: Enhancing the Lessons of Experience* by Richard Hughes and Robert Ginnett. I particularly like *The Art and Science of Leadership* by Afsaneh Nahavandi, a shorter and more interpretive text.

In Depth

There are hundreds, if not thousands of books providing guidance on the skills and qualities needed for leadership, some based in scholarship and some based in practical experience. In the former group, one of the most popular books over the last 20 years has been Kouzes and Posner's *The Leadership Challenge*. Kouzes and Posner offer five sets of behaviors that contribute to effective leadership: modeling the way, inspiring a shared vision, challenging the process, enabling others to act, and encouraging the heart.

Additionally, you might look at *The Practice of Leadership* by Jay Conger and Ronald Riggio; *The Practice of Adaptive Leadership* by Ron Heifetz, Alexander Grashow, and Marty Linsky; *The Three Faces of Leadership* by Mary Jo Hatch, Monika Kostera, and Andrzej K. Kozminski; *Why Should Anyone Be Led by You?* by Rob Goffee and Gareth Jones; and *The Extraordinary Leader* by John Zenger and Joseph Folkman. Typical of these books is a list of core competencies for leadership such as those presented by Zenger and Folkman: character, personal capability, interpersonal skills, focus on results, and leading organizational change.

A similar book, though one with an emphasis on leadership development, is *The High Potential's Advantage* by Jay Conger and Allan Church. One of the few books that examines the risks and rewards of leadership is *Leadership on the Line* by Ronald Heifetz and Marty Linsky. To complement the study of leaders, some have studied followers. See Barbara Kellerman, *Followership*. In *Leading Up*, Michael Useem describes how followers can influence leaders.

Scholars have studied exemplary leaders, but some have also studied bad leaders (appropriately, since we've all encountered some). See Barbara Kellerman's *Bad Leadership*, and Jean Lipman-Bluman's *The Allure of Toxic Leaders*.

Among those books providing potential leaders with guidance based on experience, there are many biographies and historical studies of specific leaders, from Ghandi to Hitler and beyond. Of course, there are also many biographies of United States presidents available. Recently, Doris Kearns Goodwin brought together lessons about leadership from previous studies of American presidential leadership in her book, *Leadership in Turbulent Times*. The book focuses on leadership lessons drawn from the lives of Abraham Lincoln, Theodore Roosevelt, Franklin Roosevelt, and Lyndon Johnson. Similarly, Stanley McChrystal's book *Leaders* studies the lives of pairs of leaders such as Martin Luther and Martin Luther King Jr.

A number of corporate executives and military leaders have authored reflections on their leadership experiences and the lessons they learned from those experiences. These include Max DePree's *Leadership Jazz* and *Leadership is an Art*, various works on "servant leadership," emanating from Robert Greenleaf's initial essay, *The Servant as Leader* and his elaboration of the concept in *Servant Leadership*, Bill George's *Authentic Leadership* and *True North*, John Maxwell's *Five Levels of Leadership*, and among the most recent and powerful of books in this genre, my favorites are Bob Chapman's *Everybody Matters* and General Stanley Chrystal's *Teams of Teams*.

A number of highly practical contributions have come from executive coaches, consultants, columnists, and bloggers. Perhaps most well recognized is Marshall Goldsmith's book *What Got You Here Won't get You There*. He also wrote book called *Triggers*. Others in this genre include Simon Sinek's *Start with Why* and *Leaders Eat Last*, Patrick Lencioni's *Five Dysfunctions of a Team*, and Marcus Buckingham's *First, Break All the Rules*.

Two Classic Leadership Scholars

There are two earlier leadership scholars whose work is so substantial and so challenging that it has stood the test of time. I think any serious student of leadership must confront their ideas.

James MacGregor Burns

James MacGregor Burns, a political historian, published his classic book, *Leadership*, in 1978 (more recent and somewhat more accessible is his *Transforming Leadership*). Burns discusses leadership as a relationship between leaders and followers which can either be transactional or transformational. Transactional leadership is much like what we have described here; it is based on a rational exchange of values between and among the parties. Transformational leadership, on the other hand, is permeated by ethical considerations. Burns writes, "The function of (transformational) leadership is to engage followers, not merely to activate them, to commingle needs and aspirations and goals in a common enterprise, and in the process to make better citizens of both leaders and followers" (Burns, 1978, p. 461).

Warren Bennis

We should also make special mention of the work of Warren Bennis, whose contributions to the study of leadership over the years have been significant. Anything by Bennis is worth reading, but I would particularly point out his classics, *On Becoming a Leader*, and Bennis and Burt Nanus', *Leaders*. See also *The Essential Bennis*. Especially relevant to our work here is Bennis' book (written with Robert Taylor) entitled *Geeks and Geezers*, an analysis of generational differences in leadership. You might also be interested in the more recent book, by Bennis and Stephen B. Sample, called *The Art and Adventure of Leadership*. In his classic phrase, often repeated, though in several variations, Bennis famously held that "Managers do things right. Leaders do the right things."

More Specific Topics

Emotional Intelligence – One contemporary theme in leadership studies concerns the role of *emotional intelligence* in organizational life. This was first brought to the attention of leadership scholars with the book *Primal Leadership*, authored by Daniel Goleman, Richard Boyatis, and Annie McKee. The same authors then published *The New Leaders*, and later Boyatis and McKee wrote *Resonant Leadership*. These books, and others drawn from this work, share a common interest in the art of relationship building, something they consider indispensable in the modern age. A more recent book elaborating the emotional underpinnings of leadership is Brené Brown's *Dare to Lead*.

Personal and Organizational Learning – A group of scholars and practitioners loosely tied to the early work of Peter Senge on organizational learning has explored leadership in organizations from a personal standpoint. These include *Presence*, by Senge and several colleagues, Scharmer's *Theory U*, and Scharmer and Kaufer's *Leading from the Emerging Future*.

Leadership Skills – Several books support our argument that leadership development requires not only acquiring new skills, but changing your way of thinking and being, your overall consciousness. These include Robert Quinn's, *Building the Bridge as You Walk on It*, 2004, in which he argues that "the foundation of leadership is not thinking, behavior, competencies, techniques, or position. The foundation of leadership is who we are." Similarly, Bill Joiner and Steve Joseph contend in *Leadership Agility* that obtaining high levels of mastery is not just a matter of skill acquisition but requires a change in our consciousness. The same theme is woven throughout Bill Torbert's *Action Inquiry*, Robert Kegan's work, especially *Immunity to Change* (with Lisa Lahey), and Prasad Kaipa's *From Smart to Wise*.

The Ethics of Leadership – Different views of the ethics of leadership are contained in the book edited by Deborah Rhode, *Moral Leadership*. You should also look for Terry Price's *Leadership Ethics* and Joanne Ciulla's, *The Ethics of Leadership*. An especially interesting take on ethical behavior throughout organizations is found in Joseph Badarocco's *Leading Quietly* and in Debra Meyerson's *Tempered Radicals*. But for the best and most compact summary of the ethics of leadership in an easy-to-read style, take a look at Craig Johnson's *Meeting the Ethical Challenges of Leadership*.

Change – Books that explore the subtle (and sometimes not so subtle) dynamics of change in contemporary settings include several by John Kotter, especially *Leading Change*, *A Sense of Urgency*, and *Accelerate*. You might also enjoy *Leading Change* by James O'Toole, as well as those books noted earlier by Kegan and by Quinn. Change is also studied at the micro level: see *Tribal Leadership* by Dave Logan and others and a classic book from the Arbinger Institute, *Leadership and Self-Deception*.

Organizational Culture – The concept of organizational culture has been employed in a variety of studies of change. The classic foundation for this work was a book by Edgar Schein called *Organizational Culture and Leadership*. Jim Collins used the culture framework in the very popular *Good to Great*. Lee Bolman and Terrance Deal suggest four frames for viewing the organization's culture in *Reframing Organizations*, while Kim S. Cameron and Robert E. Quinn have explored *Diagnosing and Changing Organizational Culture*. The notion that organizational change requires personal growth is reviewed in Dal Fisher's book (with David Rooke and Bill Torbert), *Personal and Organizational Transformation through Action Inquiry*.

Women and Minorities – For insights into the challenges women and minorities face in developing their leadership, you might look at Sally Helgesen's early and excellent book, *The Female Advantage*, Barbara Kellerman's *Women and Leadership*, Shoya Zichy's book, *Women and the Leadership Q*, and, most recently, Sally Helgesen and Marshall Goldsmith's *How Women Rise*. And it's hard to talk about women and leadership without mentioning Sheryl Sandberg's popular book, *Lean In*. To understand the dynamics of blacks and whites in organizational leadership, I found *Leading in Black and White* by Ancilla Livers and Keith Caver extremely helpful.

Alternatives to Hierarchy – The search for alternatives to traditional hierarchical organization has produced a number of significant works, including Bob Chapman's, *Everybody Matters*, Clay Shirky's *Here Comes Everybody*, notable for its subtitle *The Power of Organizing without Organizations*, Frederic Laloux's *Reinventing Organizations*, Stephen Denning's book, *The Leader's Guide to Radical Management*, and Gary Hamel's *What Happens Now*.

Leadership and the Arts – Several authors have explored leadership through the lens of aesthetics, particularly Donna Ladkin, *Rethinking Leadership*, Michael Jones, *Artful Leadership*, and a book I wrote with Janet Denhardt, titled *The Dance of Leadership*. Especially accessible is Frank Barett's *Say Yes to the Mess*.

BIBLIOGRAPHY AND WORKS CITED

Abbott, Edwin. *Flatland* (originally published in 1884). Dover Publications, 2012.
Arbinger Institute (eds.). *Leadership and Self Deception: Getting Out of the Box*. Berrett-Koehler, 2000.
Badaracco, Joseph Jr. *Leading Quietly: An Unorthodox Guide to Doing the Right Thing*. Harvard Business School Press, 2002.
Barnard, Chester I. *The Functions of the Executive*. Harvard University Press, 1948.
Barrett, Frank. *Say Yes to the Mess: Surprising Leadership Lessons from Jazz*. Harvard Business Review Press, 2012.
Bauman, Zygmunt, *Liquid Modernity*. Polity Press, 2000.
Bennis, Warren G.. *On Becoming a Leader*, 4th ed. Perseus Press, 2009.
Bennis, Warren G. *The Essential Bennis*. Jossey-Bass, 2015.
Bennis, Warren G. and Burt Nanus. *Leaders: The Strategies for Taking Charge*, 2nd ed. Harper Business, 2007.
Bennis, Warren and Stephen B. Sample. *The Art and Adventure of Leadership*. Wiley, 2015.
Bennis, Warren G. and Robert J. Thomas. *Geeks and Geezers.* Harvard Business Review Press, 2002.
Bolman, Lee and Terrence Deal. *Reframing Organizations: Artistry, Choice, and Leadership*. Jossey-Bass, 2000.
Boyatzis, Richard and Annie McKee. *Resonant Leadership: Renewing Yourself and Others with Mindfulness, Hope and Compassion*. Harvard Business School Press, 2005.
Brown, Brené. *Dare to Lead: Brave Work, Tough Conversations, Whole Hearts*. Random House, 2018.
Buckingham, Marcus. *First, Break All the Rules: What the World's Greatest Managers Do Differently*. Gallup Press, 2016.
Burns, James MacGregor. *Leadership*. Harper Torchbooks, 1978.
Burns, James MacGregor. *Transforming Leadership*. Atlantic Monthly Press, 2003.
Cameron, Kim S. and Robert E. Quinn. *Diagnosing and Changing Organizational Culture: The Competing Values Framework*. Jossey-Bass, 2011.
Campbell, Joseph. *The Hero with a Thousand Faces*. Princeton University Press, 1973.

Chapman, Robert and Rajk Sisodia. *Everybody Matters: The Extraordinary Power of Caring for Your People like Family*. Portfolio, 2015.
Ciulla, Joanne. *The Ethics of Leadership*. Cengage, 2002.
Collins, Jim. *Good to Great: Why Some Companies Make the Leap and Others Don't*. Harper Business, 2001.
Conger, Jay and Allan Church. *The High Potential's Advantage: Get Noticed, Impress Your Bosses, and Become a Top Leader*. Harvard Business Review Press, 2018.
Conger, Jay A. and Ronald E. Riggio. *The Practice of Leadership*. Jossey-Bass, 2006.
Cronin, Thomas and Eugene Genovese: *Leadership Matters: Unleashing the Power of Paradox*. Paradigm Publishing, 2012.
Denhardt, Robert B. *In the Shadow of Organization*. University Press of Kansas, 1981.
Denhardt, Robert B. *The Pursuit of Significance*. Waveland Press, 2000.
Denhardt, Robert B. *Just Plain Good Management*. New Insight Publishers, 2014.
Denhardt, Robert B. and Janet V. Denhardt, *The Dance of Leadership: The Art of Leading in Business, Government, and Society*. M. E. Sharpe, 2006.
Denning, Stephen. *The Leader's Guide to Radical Management: Reinventing the Workplace for the 21st Century*. Jossey-Bass, 2010.
DePree, Max. *Leadership Is an Art*. Doubleday, 1989.
DePree, Max. *Leadership Jazz*, rev. ed. Crown Business, 2008.
Fisher, Delmar, Mark Rooke, and Bill Torbert, *Personal and Organizational Transformation through Action Inquiry*. Edge/Work Press, 2001.
George, Bill. *Authentic Leadership: Rediscovering the Secrets to Creating Lasting Value*. Jossey-Bass. 2004.
George, Bill with Peter Sims. *True North*. Jossey-Bass, 2007.
Goffee, Rob and Gareth Jones. *Why Should Anyone Be Led by You? What It Takes to Be an Authentic Leader*. Knopf, 2006.
Goldsmith, Marshall. *What Got You Here Won't Get You There: How Successful People Become Even More Successful*. Profile Books, 2013.
Goldsmith, Marshall. *Triggers: Creating Behavior That Lasts – Becoming the Person You Want to Be*. Crown Business, 2015.
Goleman, Daniel, Richard Boyatzis, and Annie McKee. *Primal Leadership: Realizing the Power of Emotional Intelligence*. Harvard University Press, 2002.
Goleman, Daniel, Richard Boyatzis, and Annie McKee. *The New Leaders. Transforming the Art of Leadership into the Science of Results*. Times Warner Books UK, 2003. Little-Brown, 2006.
Greenleaf, Robert. *Servant Leadership: A Journey into the Nature of Legitimate Power and Greatness*, anniv. ed. Paulist Press, 2012.
Greenleaf, Robert. *The Servant as Leader*, rev. ed. Greenleaf Center for Servant Leadership, 2015.
Habermas, Jürgen. *Knowledge and Human Interests*. Jeremy Shapiro trans. Beacon Press, 1997.
Hagman, George. *Aesthetic Experience*. Rodopi, 2011.
Hamel, Gary. *What Matters Now: How to Win in a World of Relentless Change, Ferocious Competition, and Unstoppable Innovation*. Jossey-Bass, 2012.
Hatch, Mary Jo, Monika Kostera, and Andrzej K. Kozminski. *The Three Faces of Leadership: Manager, Artist, Priest*. Blackwell Publishing, 2005.
Hegel, Georg Wilhelm Friedrich (originally published in 1824). *Reason in History: A General Introduction to the Philosophy of History*. Liberal Arts Press, 1953.

Heifetz, Ronald, Alexander Grashow, and Marty Linsky. *The Practice of Adaptive Leadership.* Harvard Business School Press, 2009.
Heifetz, Ronald and Marty Linsky. *Leadership on the Line: Staying Alive through the Dangers of Leading,* rev. ed. Harvard University Press, 2017.
Helgesen, Sally. *The Female Advantage.* Crown Publishing, 2011.
Helgesen, Sally and Marshall Goldsmith. *How Women Rise.* Hatchett Books, 2018.
Hughes, Richard L. and Robert C. Ginnett. *Leadership: Enhancing the Lessons of Experience,* 8th ed. McGraw-Hill, 2014.
Johnson, Craig E. *Meeting the Ethical Challenges of Leadership: Casting Light or Shadow,* 6th ed. Sage Publications, 2017.
Joiner, Bill and Steve Josephs. *Leadership Agility: Five Levels of Mastery for Anticipating and Initiating Change.* Jossey-Bass, 2007.
Jones, Michael. *Artful Leadership: Awakening the Commons of the Imagination.* Trafford Publishers, 2006.
Jung, Carl. *Symbols of Transformation* (vol. 2). Harper & Brothers, 1962.
Jung, Carl. *Psychological Types,* 3rd ed. Princeton University Press, 1971.
Kaipa, Prasad and Navi Radjou. *From Smart to Wise: Acting and Leading with Wisdom.* Jossey-Bass, 2013.
Kearns Goodwin, Doris. *Leadership in Turbulent Times.* Simon and Schuster, 2018.
Kegan, Robert and Lisa Lahey. *Immunity to Change.* Harvard Business Press, 2009.
Kellerman, Barbara. *Bad Leadership: What It Is, How It Happens, Why It Matters.* Harvard Business School Press, 2004.
Kellerman, Barbara. *Followership: How Followers Are Creating Change and Changing Leaders.* Harvard Business Review Press, 2008.
Kellerman, Barbara (ed.). *Leadership.* McGraw-Hill, 2010.
Kellerman, Barbara and Deborah L. Rhode. *Women and Leadership: The State of Play and Strategies for Change.* Jossey-Bass, 2007.
Kotter, John P. *A Sense of Urgency.* Cambridge: Harvard Business Review Press, 2008.
Kotter, John P. *Accelerate.* Cambridge: Harvard Business Review Press, 2008.
Kotter, John P. *Leadership: Essential Selections on Leadership Power and Influence.* McGraw-Hill, 2010.
Kotter, John P. *Leading Change.* Updated with a new preface by the author. Harvard Business Review Press, 2012.
Kouzes, James and Barry Posner. *The Leadership Challenge,* 6th ed. Jossey-Bass, 2017.
Kuhn, Thomas. *The Structure of Scientific Revolutions,* 4th ed. The University of Chicago Press, 2015.
Ladkin, Donna. *Rethinking Leadership: A New Look at Old Leadership Questions.* Edward Elgar, 2011.
Laloux, Frederic. *Reinventing Organizations.* Nelson Parker, 2014.
Lencioni, *Five Dysfunctions of a Team.* Jossey-Bass, 2002.
Lipman-Blumen, Jean. *Connective Leadership.* Oxford University Press, 2000.
Lipman-Blumen, Jean. *The Allure of Toxic Leaders. Why We Follow Destructive Bosses and Corrupt Politicians – and How We Can Survive Them.* Oxford University Press, 2006.
Livers, Ancella and Keith Caver. *Leading in Black and White: Working Across the Racial Divide in Corporate America.* Jossey-Bass, 2007.
Logan, Dave. John King, and Halley Fischer. *Tribal Leadership.* Harper-Collins, 2009.
Marcuse, Herbert. *An Essay on Liberation.* Beacon Press, 1971.
Maxwell, John C. *The Five Levels of Leadership: Proven Steps to Maximize Your Potential.* Center Street Publishers, 2013.

McChrystal, Stanley. *Team of Teams: New Rules of Engagement for Complex World*. Portfolio Books, 2015.
McChrystal, Stanley. *Leaders: Myth and Reality*. Portfolio Books, 2018.
Meyerson, Debra. *Tempered Radicals: How People Use Difference to Inspire Change at Work*. Harvard Business School Press, 2001.
Nahavandi, Afsaneh. *The Art and Science of Leadership*, 7th ed. Pearson, 2014.
Northouse, Peter G. *An Introduction to Leadership: Concepts and Practice*, 8th ed. Sage Publications, 2012.
Northouse, Peter G. *Leadership: Theory and Practice*, 8th ed. Sage Publications, 2019.
O'Toole, James. *Leading Change: The Argument for Values-Based Leadership*. Ballentine Books, 1996.
Palmer, Parker. *Let Your Life Speak: Listening for the Voice of Vocation*. John Wiley & Sons, Inc., 2000.
Pfeffer, Jeffrey. *Power: Why Some People Have it and Others Don't*. Harper Collins, 2010.
Price, Terry L. *Leadership Ethics: An Introduction*. Cambridge University Press, 2008.
Quinn, Robert E. *Building the Bridge as You Walk on It: A Guide for Leading Change*. Jossey-Bass, 2004.
Rhode, Deborah L. (ed.). *Moral Leadership. The Theory and Practice of Power, Judgment and Policy*. Jossey-Bass, 2007.
Sandberg, Sheryl. *Lean In: Women, Work, and the Will to Lead*. Knopf, 2013.
Scharmer, C. Otto. *Theory U*. Society for Organizational Learning, 2007.
Scharmer, Otto and Katrin Kaeufer. *Leading from the Emerging Future*. Barrett Koehler Publishers, 2013.
Schein, Edgar. *Organizational Culture and Leadership*, 5th ed. Jossey-Bass, 2016.
Senge, Peter, Joseph Jaworski, Otto Scharmer, and Betty Sue Flowers. *Presence*. Cambridge, MA: Society for Organizational Learning, 2004.
Senge, P., B. Smith, Laur, J. Kruschwitz, and S. Schley. *The Necessary Revolution: How Individuals and Organizations Are Working Together to Create a Sustainable World*. Doubleday, 2008.
Shirky, Clay. *Here Comes Everybody: The Power of Organizing without Organizations*. London: Penguin Press, 2008.
Sinek, Simon. *Start with Why*. Portfolio, 2009.
Sinek, Simon. *Leaders Eat Last*. Portfolio, 2014.
Stangis, Dave and Katherine Valvoda Smith. *21st Century Corporate Citizenship*. Emerald Publishing Ltd., 2017.
Taylor, Frederick. *The Principles of Scientific Management* (originally published in 1911). Cosimo Classics, 2010.
Torbert, Bill and Associates. *Action Inquiry – The Secret of Timely and Transformational Leadership*. Berrett-Koehler, 2004.
Useem, Michael. *Leading Up: How to Lead Your Boss So You Both Win*. Crown Publishing, 2001.
Yukl, Gary. *Leadership in Organizations*, 8th ed. Pearson, 2012.
Zenger, John and Joseph Folkman. *The Extraordinary Leader: Turning Good Managers into Great Leaders*. McGraw Hill, 2002.
Zichy, Shoya. *Women and the Leadership Q: Revealing the Four Paths to Influence and Power*. McGraw-Hill, 2000.

ACKNOWLEDGMENTS

Five of the last six years, as Director of Leadership Programs at the University of Southern California's Price School of Public Policy, I directed the Executive Master of Leadership program and co-directed an Executive Leadership Development Program for Los Angeles County. These experiences changed my perspective on leadership, maybe even changed my life.

While I had taught leadership and management for many years prior to that, working intensely with these young aspiring leaders and a superb faculty gave me a new appreciation for the depth of commitment required for effective and rewarding leadership. I especially learned what a personal experience leadership is, and that the best leadership is not simply a collection of skills and strategies but comes from deep within.

In EML, we managed to create a climate of trust and camaraderie in each cohort that led to self-discovery and personal growth based in healthy human relationships.

In the ELDP, we were able to create extraordinary collaboration between the university and the county that was manifest in the classroom through a remarkable commitment to innovation and service.

In both programs I learned from my colleagues, partners, and most of all my students. I've tried to capture the spirit of these conversations in the lessons shared here.

There are many people who deserve my thanks and I'll mention a few.

I first want to thank Dean Jack Knott for giving me the opportunity to explore leadership in the classroom and beyond, during my time at USC.

My closest colleagues in running EML were Rick Culley and Rosana Padilla-Martinez. Rick, one of the country's leading executive coaches and consultants, co-anchored the classroom sessions with me, and brought his immense process skills to the conduct of the class. Rosana Padilla-Martinez is one of the best administrators I've seen in a lifetime of teaching management and administration. She also introduced me to two delightful young women, Ruby and Emma, her daughters, whom I often think of as the vanguard of the new leadership.

Paul Danczyk, Tommy Royston, and Mira Ringler, have been great colleagues and have joined with me in a remarkable partnership with Lisa Garrett, Epi Peinado, and others in LA County in developing an award-winning program which has now touched the lives of over 350 County employees. What fun!

Both personal support and intellectual encouragement came from Don and Cyndi Cutler, Tom Catlaw and Suzanne Fallender, Joe Manes and Tommy Royston, and Orion White and Cynthia McSwain. They have combined to keep me relatively sane and have also contributed many important ideas held within these pages.

Among my academic colleagues, I especially appreciated time spent talking about leadership with Tara Blanc, Tom Catlaw, Juliet Musso, Afsaneh Nahavandi, Chet Newland, Jeff Raffel, Kelly Rawlings, and Dan Rich.

Several folks deserve special comments for their help in shaping this project. Early on, I benefited from many conversations with my very wise friend Prasad Kaipa. Laree Keily is a management consultant, facilitator, speaker, and writer – and her presentations are so eloquent they make my head hurt. I also very much appreciated Jeanette Winters' erudite presentations and enjoyed our less-than-erudite conversations. Lorraine Aguilar not only presented in EML but joined in the band. More recently, I have benefited from the fresh insight and guidance of Renee Smith. Thanks to all!

Music and musicians played a major role in changing my perspectives on leadership. Dan Crary is a national treasure, the best flatpick guitarist in the world, well known in bluegrass music, but skilled in many other genres, now including teaching leadership. John and Gloria Burgess have taught me a great deal through their friendship, their musical spirit, and their sheer presence. I met Martin and Teresa Shinn at a jazz club in Los Angeles. In addition to his day job, Martin is a superb jazz guitarist and he became complicit in my attempts to communicate leadership through music in the classroom. Ron McCurdy, a wonderful teacher of jazz and leadership, even allowed me to sing with his quartet!

David Seid is in a special category having worked with me on *Just Plain Good Management* and having helped me navigate the publishing world since.

Carol Geffner is carrying on the tradition of EML. The program is in good hands.

Rueben Brock was especially helpful in discussing his work on African-American leadership development. Morgan Vogel of Nebraska Omaha also read the full manuscript and provided very helpful comments.

All of my students contributed to my enhanced understanding of leadership, most without even knowing they were doing so. But I want to give a special shout-out to David Esterson, Kimhan Doan, Jim Featherstone, Quentin Foster, Mike Gebhart, Steve Goldfarb, Yesenia Gutierrez, Laura Herren, and my two favorite students – they know who they are.

Cari Denhardt and Mary Goodman talked with me at length about young women seeking leadership while they lived the struggle. They joined with Ben and Michael in our exploration of the complexities of leadership in families, specifically ours.

My special thanks to Amy Harris who worked with me on early versions of the manuscript, and, of course, my Taylor & Francis editor Meredith Norwich, who provided guidance and encouragement and just the right amount of push, and her assistant Mary del Plato, who steered the book through to its publication. Their work was very much appreciated.

Finally, I want to thank my wife, Janet, who has been a great colleague, a (usually) correct critic, an outstanding co-author, and an enthusiastic co-conspirator throughout our time at Arizona State University and now at the University of Southern California. But more importantly, she has been a marvelously caring and compassionate partner in life and love. We made it!

Bob

INDEX

action 20, 48; and leadership 25, 31–2, 43, 45, 159
adaptability 68, 154
African-Americans 113–15
age differences 6, 9–10, 13–15; leadership 86–7, 147; *see also* millennials
agility 44, 68, 89
ambition 16, 58, 63, 98
the arts 77, 155–8
authenticity 97, 111, 126–7
authority 57, 97; *see also* power
autonomy 14–15, 91–2, 101, 126–7; autonomous collaboration 90

behavioral approaches 33, 108
beliefs 69, 125–6, 129
Bennis, Warren 13, 169
Blanchard, Angela 69
Boyd, Dinah 70
Burns, James MacGregor 48, 169
Bush, George H.W. 66

calmness 44, 52–3, 148
capacity 101–2, 104–5, 110, 146
change 44; of leadership model 126–31; organizational change 33–4, 37, 89, 128–9, 130; social change 14, 91–2, 101, 153
chaotic organizations 69, 89
charisma 18, 48
Clinton, Bill 111
Clinton, Hillary 111

coercion 98–102, 103–4, 110, 126, 146
collaboration 91, 100, 101–2, 104–5; autonomous collaboration 90
communication 35, 64, 104–5; empathetic communication 76–7, 105; listening 33–4, 41, 108, 117; and power 100; problems 57, 58; skills 74–7; supportive communication 76–7, 105
communities 101–2, 104–5, 133, 149; black 122
consumer behavior 117
Cooper, Martin 34–6
craftsmanship 102–3
creativity 45, 132–3, 155, 156–7
crises 128–9
culture 86, 115, 117–18, 157–8; beliefs 125–6; cultural awareness 154–5; organizational 7, 58

democratic enquiry 29
digital world 13–14, 88, 129–30
direction 31, 68–71
discrimination 49, 107, 119, 123; racial 113–16, 122
diversity 113–18, 121–3, 155; *see also* inclusion

economic performance 15–16, 87, 90
ego 16, 43, 98
emotional intelligence 27, 34, 42, 44–5, 74
empathy 74–5, 82, 126; empathetic communication 76–7, 105

Index

energy 42, 46–7, 52–3, 117–18; energizing 25–8, 31, 33, 100, 106, 130, 157, 161; exchange 50; moral energy 42, 47–9, 136; personal energy 42, 43–4, 136; social energy 42, 44–7, 136
engagement 31, 34, 43, 101, 117–18; of the group 25, 58, 157
environmental impacts 15–16, 90, 93
ethics 15, 93, 129–30; and leadership 16, 47–8, 126, 142; use of power 99
ethnic minorities: African-Americans 113–15; Latinas 115–16
exchanges *see* transactions
executive coaches 51, 55, 138
executive functions *see* management

feminine principle 110–11
fiscal performance 15–16, 87, 90

gendered leadership myth 108, 109–10, 112; *see also* women
generational differences *see* age differences
groups 27; engagement 25, 58; leadership 26–7, 28, 77–8

Habermas, Jürgen 92
hard skills 72–3, 87
Hegel, G.W. F. 91–2
hero myths 142
Hitler, Adolf 47, 48
home environment 21–2, 65, 151

identity 17, 70, 114
imposter syndrome 109–10
inclusion 102, 116–18; *see also* diversity
individuals 28; in groups 45–6, 50; and power 100, 102; rights 99, 122
individuation 87, 89, 146
inducements 80–1, 86, 90–1, 98
inequality 16, 90–1
intuition 34, 91–2, 145–6

job changes 11, 21–2, 24, 65, 95, 149–50; *see also* personal development
Jung, Carl 87

Kayla: personal life 151–2; work situation 5–8, 19, 50–1, 137–8, 147–8
Kellerman, Barbara 3
Kennedy, John 46
Kerle, Ralph 69
Kim 55–7, 59, 61–4
King, Martin Luther 70–1

Latinas 115–16
leaders, roles 41–2
leadership 54–5; the art of 154–9; demands of 117–18, 132–4; and management 25–6, 33, 88, 100; nature of 3, 12–13, 18, 20–1; new formulation 25–7, 88–9, 100–6, 117–18, 126–31, 145–6, 149; and power 25–6, 48, 96–102; responsibilities of 68–9; rewards of 134–6; traditional model 2, 15–16, 27, 97–8, 124–6, 145–6, 153; *see also* organizations
leadership journey 141–4, 151–2, 159–60
leadership moment 30–2, 35, 39–40, 76
leading, acts of 26–7, 30, 132–3
listening 41, 117; skills 74, 76, 108
love 104, 126

male perspective 107, 121–2
management 37, 45, 72–3, 98; and leadership 25–6, 33, 88, 100; *see also* organizations; planning
marginalized groups *see* minority groups
Mari 28–30
masculine principle 110–11
mentorship 19, 51
Mike: job changes 11, 21–2, 24, 65, 95, 149–50; personal life 21–2, 152; self-discovery 11; work situation 83–4
millennials 6, 9–10, 13–15, 51, 119; relationships 81; *see also* age differences
minority groups 107; discrimination 113–16; ethnic minorities 113–16, 122–3
moral energy 42, 47–9, 136
moral issues 142–3; *see also* ethics
moral responsibility 103, 112

narrative 31–2, 33–4, 41, 45, 77–8, 156–7
networks 111–12
nonprofit organizations 95

Obama, Barack 111
Obama, Michelle 111
observation: energy flows 52–3; power relationships 19
organizations: culture 7, 58; ethical behaviour 93–4; of the future 16–17, 64, 89–91; leadership in 54–5; organizational change 33–4, 37, 128–9, 130; power structures 15, 57–60; rational model 80–1; spatial representation 105; transactional nature 59–60, 63–4, 86, 88; *see also* leadership; management

pace 156–7
pattern recognition 31, 45, 76, 78–9
personal development 95, 137–8, 139–41, 145–6; direction 12–13; leadership 89; roadblocks 12, 19, 21, 113–16, 138; self-awareness 21; *see also* job changes
personal life 16–17, 21–2, 129–30
personal qualities 43–4, 84, 87, 156; leadership qualities 13, 42, 135–6, 160; personal energy 42, 43–4, 136
personalization 89–90
Pfeffer, Jeffrey 97–8
planning 67–8, 70–1, 81, 84; *see also* management
playground leadership 28–30
politics 97
power 17, 64, 88, 94, 122; bias 116–17; as capacity 101–2, 104–5, 110, 146; as coercion 98–102, 103–4, 110, 126, 146; and leadership 25–6, 48, 96–8; in organizations 15, 57–60; women 110–12; *see also* authority
praxis 20, 45
presence (leader's) 102, 110–11
purpose 31, 68–71

racism 113–16, 122
reflection 20, 45; self-reflection 42, 70, 123, 161
reflexivity 70
relationships 118; building 28, 31; deterioration of 83–4; and leadership 26, 45–6, 48, 50, 54; maintenance of healthy 55–60, 61–4, 89; millennials 81; and transactions 81, 87, 104–5
resilience 43
responsibilities 68–9, 103, 133
rewards of leadership 134–6
rhythm 156–7
roadblocks 12, 19, 21, 113–16, 138
Robert 5, 12, 19, 50–1, 137–8, 147–8

self-awareness 21, 43, 143–4
self-confidence 19, 24, 43, 98
self-discovery 11, 85, 87, 139–41, 145–6
self-reflection 42, 70, 123, 161

settings 28, 54
sexism 7–8, 24, 109, 116, 120, 148
situational leadership 153
skills 76–8, 82, 102–3, 160–1; communications 33, 74, 75, 76–7, 108; hard skills 72–3, 87; soft skills 72–3, 74, 75, 87, 108; squishy skills 74–5, 82, 87, 89, 108–9
slavery 97, 122
social change 14, 91–2, 101, 153
social energy 42, 44–7, 136
social impacts 15–16, 90
soft skills 72–3, 74, 75, 87, 108
soul 43, 158–9
sports 46, 83–4; sportsmanship 103
squishy skills 74–5, 82, 87, 89, 108–9
standing (leader's) 31, 32, 33, 35, 111, 133
stereotypes 114–16, 122; age differences 6, 9–10, 51
supportive communication 76–7
sustainability 90, 93, 127, 144; of leadership 32–4

Taylor, Frederick 72
teams *see* groups
technology 13–14, 88, 129–30
trait theories 32
transactions 45, 80–1, 99, 117, 118; in organizations 17, 59–60, 63–4, 74, 80–1, 87, 88, 99

universities 34–6, 126–7

values 47, 69–70, 103–4, 140–1, 142–3
visibility 111
vision 39, 70–1, 81–2, 88; and leadership 18, 25–6, 35–6; setting 66–8
vulnerability 24, 63

women 119–20, 121–2; discrimination against 107; Latinas 115–16; leadership 108–12; roles at work 23–4
work environment 14–15, 129–30
work-life balance 21–2, 24–5, 129–30, 144, 151–2